THE NEW ITALIAN COOKBOOK

Joanne Glynn

PHOTOGRAPHY BY ROWAN FOTHERINGHAM
STYLING BY DONNA HAY

BayBooks
An imprint of HarperCollinsPublishers

STOCKISTS

Art of Stone
159 Old South Head Road
Edgecliff NSW
Tel: (02) 363 3232
(Also Mosman)

Aviamentos
Ribbons and Braids
457 King Street
Newtown NSW
Tel: (02) 550 3774

Bibelot
445 Oxford Street
Paddington NSW
Tel: (02) 360 6902
(Also North Sydney)

Chris Savage & Associates
Decorative Plaster
71 John Street
Leichardt
Tel: (02) 692 0922

Corso de Fiori
35 South Dowling Street
Darlinghurst NSW
Tel: (02) 360 5151
(also Surry Hills, Chatswood,
Skygardens and Melbourne)

Cydonia the Glass Studio
Unit A2 1–3 Gladstone Street
Newtown NSW
Tel: (02) 557 5898

Glass Artists Gallery
70 Glebe Point Road
Glebe NSW
Tel: (02) 552 1552

Hale Imports
Pillivuyt
97–99 Old Pittwater Road
Brookvale NSW
Tel: (02) 938 2400

Orrefors Kosta-Boda
Shop 1033 Westfield Shopping
Centre, Miranda
Tel: (02) 524 9409
(Also Frenchs Forest, Castle Hill,
Mosman)

Terazzo & Co. Pty Ltd
5 O'Riordan Street
Alexandria NSW
Tel: (02) 319 5351

Ventura Imports
60 Justin Street
Lilyfield
Tel: (02) 555 7277

Villeroy and Boch (Aust) Pty Ltd
7 Orchard Road
Brookvale
Tel: (02) 938 5022

A BAY BOOKS PUBLICATION
An imprint of HarperCollinsPublishers

First published in Australia in 1993 by Bay Books, of

CollinsAngus&Robertson Publishers Pty Limited (ACN 009 913 517)
A division of HarperCollinsPublishers (Australia) Pty Limited
25 Ryde Road, Pymble NSW 2073, Australia
HarperCollinsPublishers (New Zealand) Limited
31 View Road, Glenfield, Auckland 10, New Zealand
HarperCollinsPublishers Limited
77-85 Fulham Palace Road, London W6 8JB, United Kingdom

Copyright © Bay Books 1993

National Library of Australia
Cataloguing-in-Publication data:

Glynn, Joanne
    The new Italian cookbook
    Includes index.
    ISBN 1 86378 061 0.
    1. Cookery, Italian. I. Title. (Series: Bay Books cookery collection).
641.5945

Photographer: Rowan Fotheringham
Food stylist: Donna Hay
Food stylist's assistant: Beth Pittman

Cover photograph: Recipes: Veal with Prosciutto and Vermouth (page 51);
Pappardelle with Sun-dried Tomatoes (page 37)
Background from Terazzo and Co.; mosaic plate from Villeroy & Boch, glass plate
from Cydonia the Glass Studio

Printed in Australia by Griffin Press Limited, Netley, South Australia

5 4 3 2 1
97 96 95 94 93

CONTENTS

~

ITALIAN REGIONAL CUISINE

It has only been since 1861 that there has existed the unified Italy we know today. It was previously made up of regions of politically independent kingdoms and states, with many of these experiencing a history of occupation which left a very strong influence on the language, lifestyle and customs. These regions had distinct geographical as well as political boundaries and the majority of the population had little inclination or ability to move out of their region. The influences of the occupying nation in the kitchens were sometimes most pronounced, and it is this, plus the produce unique to that region, which has given them each a very distinctive cuisine.

As the unified Italy became more industrial, a good transport system developed. People became more mobile and discovered cooking from regions other than their own, and in addition, local produce was able to be freighted efficiently all over the country. Inevitably, this brought about a merging of cooking styles. The traditional differences between north and south became less marked and the intermingling population and modern living has blurred the distinctions. The busy urban housewife of today in Italy is just as likely to cook uncomplicated meals using pre-prepared foods from the supermarket during the week (like the rest of us have been doing for decades), and to prepare traditional regional food for a special occasion or on weekends.

Despite this, regional food has maintained a strong identity. Great pride and rivalry exists between the cooks of neighbouring regions, and Italians love to talk about food just as much as they enjoy eating it. There is nearly always an amusing legend attached to classic dishes, and it's often not how much truth there is in these stories, but the spirit of regional pride in which they're told that counts!

Italians are great eaters-out, and there is quite a range of eating places, from bars and osterias, to trattorias and ristorantes. It is common to see restaurants full of large, happy groups, particularly for Sunday lunch, as dining out is regarded as a congenial get-together with family and friends as much as it is the enjoyment of good food. It is called *il culto del ben essere*, the pursuit of the good life!

THE REGIONS AND THEIR SPECIALITIES

SARDINIA Sardinia is the second largest Mediterranean island and is almost totally populated by fishermen on the coast and by shepherds and farmers inland. The land is rugged and the people live in a close community strongly influenced by its ancient customs. In this environment, old cooking techniques have been kept alive.

The favourite method of cooking lamb, baby goat or suckling pig (called *porceddu*) is spit-roasting over an open fire. Another outdoor cooking technique is baking the carcass in a pit covered with burning embers.

Sheep are plentiful, and a lot of ewe's milk cheese is made, which is more often than not quite strong and smelly!

On the coast the local fish stew is called *cassola,* distinguished by the large number of fish used and the addition of crab and chilli. Sardines, swordfish, tuna, eel, plus the local lobster are also very good.

The preferred pasta is spaghetti, tubular shapes or a local ravioli called *culingiones.* In fact, one of the main commercial crops of the island is durum wheat.

SICILY Sicily has had 2000 years of occupation by a large number of outsiders: Greeks and Romans, Saracens, Normans, Spanish and French among them. The food, reflecting this mixed culture, is rich, varied and intense, with strange combinations and often using many ingredients. Most cities have a distinct cuisine, while the food of the countryside is a more uniform 'poor' food. Sicilians love anything that comes from the sea, and Mediterranean fish and shellfish are a big part of the diet. Bread and pasta are important, with spaghetti being the most commonly used pasta. Fruit and vegetables are plentiful, in fact eggplants (aubergine), capsicum (peppers) and tomatoes typify the cuisine.

There is a great passion for desserts; many creations are truly elaborate and are only bought from the pasticceria to serve on grand occasions. Beautifully formed marzipan fruits and Sicilian preserved fruits are famous.

CALABRIA Calabria is the toe of the boot of Italy, and so is almost entirely surrounded by sea. Once, under Greek rule, it was rich and prosperous, but today it is very poor with the lowest per capita income in Italy. It is mountainous and rocky and the life is simple. The people live on pasta, soup, vegetables and fish. Kid, small game and some

poultry are eaten. Lamb and especially pig are celebrated and are usually saved for a special occasion. On the coast, swordfish and tuna are plentiful, and whitebait is enjoyed in any number of ways.

Cheese is eaten morning, noon and night. Capsicums (peppers), eggplants (aubergines) and mushrooms are particularly good from Calabria.

BASILICATA Basilicata was once wooded and green. Now, after years of natural and human erosion it is poor and is the least populated of the regions.

Pork products such as salamis and sausages are popular, along with poultry. Sheep are also important and are used for wool and cheese. If mutton is eaten, it is served very plainly. Wild herbs, and in particular rosemary, are used to flavour dishes in the hills. Pasta is important in the diet and is served simply, often with cheese. Dishes generally have few ingredients, but a favourite flavouring is chilli, *peperoncino,* and this appears everywhere and in everything! *Olio santo,* chillis steeped in olive oil, is served as a condiment.

APULIA Before water was brought in at the beginning of the century, Apulia had no great agricultural history.

The fresh produce grown tended to be of a type that was hardy such as olives, sheep, and vines, and this is evident in the simple traditional cooking. Wild vegetables like fennel, asparagus and onions were gathered and these are still popular along with cropped vegetables of artichokes, capsicum, eggplant and broad beans. Onions are important to the cooking, and are used more

than garlic. A lot of bread is eaten, and the stuffed pastries called *calzone* and *panzerotti* originated here. But the staple is pasta, and Apulians live, eat and dream it! Cheese is a big part of the diet and mozzarella and pecorino in particular are local institutions. There is good fishing around the long coastline and excellent shellfish, especially with the oysters and mussels from the Gulf of Taranto.

CAMPANIA The Romans called it *Campania Felix,* the happy country, and today's flamboyant Campanians are proof that things haven't changed. Naples is the heart and soul of Campania, and its tastes and styles are that of the whole region.

The cuisine is colourful and vital, just like the Campanians. Who else could have adopted the bright, sunny tomato after everyone else in Europe regarded it with deep suspicion when it was first brought by the Spanish from America in the sixteenth century. The Spanish also brought capsicum (peppers), and these too found a welcome home.

This is also the home of the pizza, made in Naples with a thin and crisp crust. Pastry making in general is important and elaborate sweet creations are bought from the pasticceria for special occasions, leaving the simpler baking for the home cook. Tubular pasta or spaghetti predominates.

The cuisine doesn't include much meat but when it does appear, it's usually pig or lamb, and frying is the cooking method of choice. As can be expected with the Bay of Naples dominating the coastline, lots of fish and shellfish are eaten, with anchovies and sardines cheap and plentiful.

ABRUZZI AND MOLISE These two regions on the Adriatic Coast were until recently united, and they share a common geography and lifestyle. The land in general is isolated and it is predominately rural. The Abruzzesi and Molisani are traditionally shepherds and farmers whose food is simple and robust.

There are a lot of pigs for pork and hams, and sausages and spicy salamis are popular. Pork liver is often used. Sheep, cattle and goats are bred, and game hunted. Vegetables are important, and those growing wild include mushrooms, asparagus, celery and fennel. Of the cultivated vegetables, capsicum are a favourite and in particular little red hot peppers called *diavolilli,* little devils, are used to flavour anything from soups to salamis.

One of the few commercial products of these regions is wheat, which is sold primarily to the pasta-making industry. Corn, olives, grape vines and fruit trees are grown, and saffron is cultivated in Abruzzi.

LAZIO Lazio or Latium is dominated by Rome, and here, if you look hard, can be found the true cooking of the region. Romans love simple, uncomplicated food, and they have a particular liking for offal called *il quinto quarto,* the fifth quarter. This is said to have sprung from the general public making use of what was left after the clergy and nobles finished with the better cuts of meat! Tripe and liver are common, and if meat is eaten it is mostly pork or lamb. *Abbacchio,* spring lamb, and *porchetta,* suckling pig, are favourites, and roast kid might be cooked for a special occasion.

The climate and soil have always been ideal for vegetable crops, and the vegetable course is important in the daily meal. The top vegetable around Rome is the artichoke and beans appear at most meals. Pasta is another favourite of the Romans, and they prefer long ribbon types such as *bucatini, spaghetti* and *fettuccine,* and similar pasta, stuffed and baked.

In keeping with the simple approach to food here, meals are generally finished off with just cheese, sweet wine and a biscuit.

MARCHE The Marche is a land of mountains and good pastures which is tranquil and beautiful, although lightly populated. The people are content and genuine, which is reflected in their food. Their cooking is determined by the seasons and what is available from month to month, such as mushrooms and wild vegetables. The main product is truffles and this region is the largest producer in Italy. Inland, sheep, cows, chickens and pigs are raised, and it was from here that *porchetta,* roast suckling pig, is supposed to have originated.

On the coast fish stews and soups are popular and the *brodetta* from Ancona, flavoured with white wine vinegar, has a friendly rivalry with the saffron flavoured *brodetta* of Porto Recanati.

UMBRIA Umbria, completely landlocked, is known as the green heart of Italy. The landscape is of rolling green hills, wooded slopes and deep, narrow valleys. It's no wonder that St Francis of Assisi found it easy to commune with nature in this beautiful and meditative land.

The food is uncomplicated, but given great style by the quality of the ingredients. Small game and game birds from the woods, freshwater fish from the streams and Lake Trasimeno, and wild vegetables are all a part of the cuisine.

Black truffles are plentiful and available to most farmers who have a truffle wood on their land, or at least a share in a commune.

The salami, cured and smoked sausages and hams, are famous and this important industry is centred around the town of Norcia. In fact the universal name in Italy for a pork butcher's shop is *norcino.*

Desserts aren't big, but bakeries sell a large variety of pastries served for special occasions.

TUSCANY Tuscany is the epitomy of the outsider's ideal Italy. It is green and picturesque with a countryside dotted with rolling hills, fortified villages and proud, rich cities. The people, descendants of the Etruscans, are also proud and rich of spirit with an independent nature and a love of the land. Their food is elegant but simple, relying on few gimmicks or fancy sauces to confuse the inherent flavours of the ingredients.

It is said that the Toscani live on beans, vegetables and beef, cooked in olive oil and washed down by Chianti! Fennel, artichokes and spinach are typical, as are herbs such as sage and rosemary.

Meat is more likely to be served plain, just fried or grilled, and although pork and poultry are popular, beef is the favourite. Offal such as tripe and liver appears frequently, and also sausages and salamis, which generally have a milder, more subtle flavour than those from other regions.

With the long coastline, seafood is good and plentiful, and freshwater fish and eels are also in good demand. Desserts are not usually eaten, but fruit, and hard biscuits such as *biscotti di prato* served with *vino santo* are a common end to the meal.

The Tuscan court of the sixteenth century was responsible for introducing restraint in the kitchens and decorum into the dining-rooms of Europe. They had a code of behaviour which frowned upon gluttony, the use of hands for eating, elbows and feet on the table, and the sharing of half-eaten food between guests and pets!

EMILIA-ROMAGNA This region is rich in natural resources, from the fertile agricultural soil of the Po Valley to the lagoons and coastline of the Adriatic Sea. Its capital, Bologna, is reputed to be the gastronomic capital of Italy. Known as *Bologna la Grassa*, the Fat One, it abounds in delicatessens and food stores. The people are known for their love of the good life and their cooking, is rich and elegant.

The region is famous for its egg pasta and tagliatelle originated in Bologna. Tortellini were supposedly invented here as well, when a smitten chef, sneaking a look at his loved one, spied her navel through the keyhole. What a chef! What a story!

Quality pork and pork products abound, such as *mortadella* from Bologna, *coppa* from Piazenza, prosciutto ham from Parma, and the stuffed boned pigs' feet called *zampone* from Modena. Modena is also the home of balsamic vinegar. The local butter is particularly creamy, but more often than not these days olive oil is combined with butter for cooking. Parmesan cheese comes from a designated area between Parma and Modena, with its production being strictly controlled by law.

On the coast is found *mistigriglia,* mixed grilled seafood, and the local fish soup or *brodetta* is particularly good. Seafood in general is important, but freshwater fish has traditionally never been so, unusual considering the size and extent of the Po River.

FRIULI VENEZIA-GIULIA This small region has had a checkered past. It belonged to Austria until the First World War, and then a large part of Venezia-Giulia was lost to Yugoslavia after World War II. The food reflects this political history, with Venezia-Giulia having a strong Eastern European influence, while Friuli has more the style of the countryside of Venetia.

The cooking of Friuli is simple with soups, beans and polenta common fare in the mountains, and pork and poultry in the plains. Sausages and hams are superior, the most famous being the air-cured hams of San Daniele.

The food of Venezia-Giulia includes goulash (known locally as *golas),* cabbage, horseradish and dumplings, and Austrian-style pastries like strudel are common.

Trieste, with its wealthy trading past, has a strong influence from Venice, but there is also a mix of other cuisines; sauerkraut and gnocchi from Austria, rice in soup with eggs and lemon juice like the Greek *avgolemono,* and pastries filled with nuts, honey and spices from the Middle East.

VENETO Venice is the main city of the Veneto but, just as it is isolated from the mainland, so its cuisine is unique and not an example of the region. For many centuries it was the most important city in the world and the Venetian Empire had trading links with parts of the world inaccessible to the rest of Europe. It became a great culinary focal point and through here much of the food previously unknown to Europe such as spices and maize, was introduced. These ingredients, most of which were expensive, were adopted first by the wealthy Venetians and became a part of their cuisine. The cuisine is primarily based on fish and shellfish from the lagoon and surrounding coastline. Rice is all important; their famous risotto is served with subtle flavourings and is preferred quite liquid. On the mainland the cooking is simple, colourful and based on rice, beans, *baccala* (salt cod) and polenta. Fish and shellfish are prevalent on the coast and there is an abundance of fresh vegetables.

The Veneti are likely to finish off a meal with a glass or two of grappa and perhaps a dipping biscuit, whereas sweets and pastries are more likely to be reserved for special occasions.

TRENTINO-ALTO ADIGE Bordered to the north by the Austrian Alps, this region is almost entirely mountainous. Alto Adige, in the north, was the South Tyrol of Austria until World War I. It is German speaking and the cooking is Tyrolean with a strong emphasis on pork and pork products. Goulash is common along with dumplings, and these come in many guises; small gnocchi, large knodel and canederli. Paprika, juniper berries and horseradish are common flavourings. Cabbage (in the form of sauerkraut) and potatoes are the main vegetables, with potatoes being put into everything, including sweets and cakes. In keeping with this starchy diet, bread is important, and strudel and doughnuts feature as desserts along with puddings and tarts. Down in Trentino the cuisine is primarily Italian. Polenta is all important and can be found made of a mixture of maize and buckwheat (*polenta nera*), or mixed with rice flour. Pasta made with buckwheat flour is also popular around Trento.

LOMBARDY This is the wealthiest of all the regions, having the commercial and industrial capital of Milano, the tourist mountains and lakes districts and the agriculturally bountiful Po Valley. The food is distinct in each of these areas. A lot of meat is consumed, and there are large herds of cattle (kept in long sheds and rarely visible) which also give butter and cheeses. Gorgonzola, Bel Paese and Mascarpone are all from Lombardy. Smoked and cured meats are a feature of the mountains, with *bresaola* (air-cured beef or horsemeat) worthy of particular mention. Rice, grown in the Po Valley, invariably appears as risotto. *Risotto Milanese*, the most famous of them all, is flavoured with saffron, a spice which has kept a strong presence in Milanese cooking.

Polenta, a product from the maize fields of the Po Valley, is plentiful and popular. There are a lot of vegetables, but they are often an accompaniment or part of a dish

rather than the more important separate course. Cakes and simple pastries are preferred over desserts.

LIGURIA Known as the Italian Riviera, Liguria has a narrow coastal strip which rises immediately into hills, so there is hardly any coastal plain. This geography has played a big part in the cuisine of the region as not a lot of crops or herds were suitable, although the climate is mild and sunny.

Its capital, Genoa, has always been a major port and was an important trading city with Spain and North Africa. The story goes that Genovese sailors got sick of seafood after long months at sea, and longed for fresh greens. Their sympathetic wives and mothers back home accommodated this craving, so creating a cuisine based on vegetables and herbs. This predominantly vegetarian diet, called *di magro*, also includes seafood but with the emphasis on shellfish. When meat is on the menu, it is more often than not veal. Pasta is important and Liguria is supposedly the birthplace of ravioli, evolved when pasta was used to envelope leftovers for sailors to take to sea. The contents were thus out of sight, and so with luck, palatable! Amongst the herbs, basil is king and its most famous use is in pesto, so-called because the ingredients are ground with a pestle (*pestare* means to pound). This sauce is used as a dressing as well as an ingredient and is the unique flavouring of many local dishes, such as *Minestrone alla Genovese*.

PIEMONTE & VALLE D'AOSTA Piemonte is mostly mountainous with rich river valleys. It was once

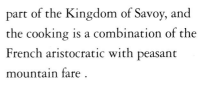

part of the Kingdom of Savoy, and the cooking is a combination of the French aristocratic with peasant mountain fare .

In the mountains, all sorts of game are eaten. Excellent cheeses are made; the alpine fondue appears as *fonduta*, made with the melting cheese Fontina. Another dipping dish from here is *bagna cauda*, a warm sauce flavoured with garlic and anchovies.

In the hills, poultry and game birds are popular, with goose being a great favourite. It is smoked, cured, made into liver pâté and turned into salami. Vineyards abound in the plains, and the wine from Piemonte is amongst the best in Italy. The Valle D'Aosta is nestled in the mountains to the northwest of Piemonte and its beautiful scenery is a great tourist attraction. It is Italy's smallest region with a per capita income which is the highest in the country. Its food, with a strong French influence, is that of the mountains of Piemonte.

STARTERS, SNACKS AND SOUPS

Bread, in many forms, is an important element in the Italian diet. In Sardinia a big variety of breads are baked. One of the favourites is thin, crisp sheets of *carta di musica*, music paper, so-called because of the crackling noise it makes when broken. Pita bread, wrapped around a variety of fillings in the Greek style, is also popular in the south, in Calabria.

Grissini, the renowned breadsticks, originate in Turin which also has a thriving confectionery and pastry-making industry.

Focaccia, stuffed with all kinds of marvels is world renowned and even *panettone,* the famous Christmas cake of Milano is actually half bread!

The Tuscans sometimes use bread as a basis for soup, while in the Veneto the most common soup, *pasta e fagioli*, is based on borlotti beans which were originally from Mexico.

On the coast fish soups are very popular. In Trieste soup often contains rice with eggs and lemon juice, like the Greek *avgolemono* and in Calabria, soup is fundamental to the relatively simple diet. Only in Basilicata, the least populated and one of the poorest regions, is soup uncommon, because there didn't used to be the abundance of vegetables found throughout the rest of Italy.

Garlic and Parmesan Grissini (page 21); Roasted Asparagus with Fontina (page 20); Linguine with Beetroot (page 23)

CAVIALE DI FUNGHI

This mushroom and pine nut 'caviar' makes an excellent topping for bruschetta or it can be used as a dip.

250 g (8 oz) mushrooms of choice

60 g (2 oz) butter

4 spring onions, finely chopped

1 clove garlic, minced

1 tablespoon dry white wine

2 tablespoons toasted pine nuts

1 tablespoon finely chopped fresh parsley

1 to 2 tablespoons sour cream

1 Chop mushrooms to give a fine but slightly chunky texture.

2 Melt butter in a frying pan and gently sauté mushrooms and spring onions for 5 minutes. Add garlic and wine and sauté 2 to 3 minutes more, or until mixture is dry. Remove from heat, cool, then stir in pine nuts and parsley. Moisten with enough sour cream to give a texture which won't break up, but which is not runny.

SERVES 4

BRUSCHETTA

Called fettunta *or* fregolotta *in Tuscany, bruschetta is old, traditional food which has been around for centuries. It was eaten by shepherds and farm workers on its own, or used as a base for a snack with a more substantial topping. Elsewhere, as in Apulia, ripe tomatoes are rubbed into the surface along with the garlic. It is still a very good way of sampling olive oil although today it is also presented more elegantly with a topping and served as an appetiser. The best bread to use is a good textured home-style oval loaf such as* pagnotti *and use the best olive oil you have.*

4 slices crusty bread, cut 1 cm (½ in) thick

2 cloves garlic, cut in half and with the green centre stem removed

extra virgin olive oil (about 4 tablespoons)

salt and freshly ground black pepper

1 Toast bread slices on both sides under a grill, or even better, over an open fire. While still hot rub one side of each slice with half a clove of garlic. Rub it in well, until most of the clove is used up. Drizzle about 1 tablespoon of oil over each slice and salt and pepper liberally. Serve hot.

SERVES 4

GORGONZOLA STICKS

1 ¼ cups (155 g/5 oz) plain (all-purpose) flour

pinch salt

¼ teaspoon paprika

cold water

60 g (2 oz) butter

60 g (2 oz) Gorgonzola cheese, or other blue vein

1 Preheat oven to 200°C (400°F) and grease a baking tray.

2 This step may be done in a food processor. Sieve flour and salt into a bowl and stir in paprika. Rub butter in well, then add cold water, a little at a time, to form a stiff dough. Knead lightly.

3 Roll out on a floured surface to a rectangle of about 3 mm (⅛ in) thick. Crumble or grate cheese evenly over half the dough. Fold over the other half to completely cover cheese.

4 Roll again over the top until quite thin and the cheese just begins to show through pastry. Trim edges with a sharp knife, then cut pastry into sticks of about 5 mm (¼ in) wide and 8 cm (3 in) long. Transfer to prepared baking tray and bake in the oven until lightly browned, about 10 minutes.

MAKES ABOUT 50 STICKS

Gorgonzola Sticks, Bruschetta with Caviale di Funghi

≈ **MORE BRUSCHETTA**

A variation on bruschetta can be made with leftover breads of many different types. Cornbread, for instance, is great when toasted and rubbed with garlic, and 2 to 3-days-old olive bread is re-born by a brush of olive oil and a minute or two on the barbecue. Even those last few slices of Christmas Panettone come into their own when toasted (with or without garlic) and served with wafer thin slices of prosciutto.

Potato, Onion and Zucchini Soup; Grilled Polenta with Gorgonzola and Walnuts

GRILLED POLENTA WITH GORGONZOLA AND WALNUTS

These little bite-sized treats make great finger food, or they can be made on a bigger scale and served individually as a starter. To clean the polenta saucepan, simply fill it with cold water and leave overnight; the crust will soak off and fall away.

POLENTA

7 cups (1¾ litres/56 fl oz) water

2⅔ cups (350 g/11 oz) polenta (cornmeal)

30 g (1 oz) butter

TOPPING

75 g (2½ oz) butter, softened

1 cup (100 g/3½ oz) walnut pieces, finely chopped

200 g (6½ oz) Gorgonzola cheese, or other creamy blue vein

thickness and smooth surface. Leave to cool and set.

2 TO PREPARE TOPPING: Blend butter, walnuts, Gorgonzola and brandy together in a bowl. Season with a few good grinds of black pepper.

3 Turn on grill to high heat.

4 With a 4 cm (1 ½ in) cookie cutter, cut out circles from the polenta. Place under grill and toast on one side. Turn over and place a good spoonful of topping on each one, then return to grill. Serve as soon as the cheese is bubbling and the walnuts slightly toasted.

SERVES 4

POTATO, ONION AND ZUCCHINI SOUP

1 tablespoon olive oil

30 g (1 oz) butter

450 g (14 oz) mild onions or leeks, sliced

2 zucchini (courgettes), sliced

450 g (14 oz) potatoes, diced

8 cups (2 litres/64 fl oz) water

pinch chilli flakes

salt

1 Melt oil and butter in a large, heavy-based saucepan and add onions. Sauté over a low heat until soft. Add zucchini, toss to coat, then sauté 1 to 2 minutes. Add potatoes and water and simmer over a low heat until potatoes are cooked and start to break down. If neccessary, increase heat to thicken, or add some more water to thin. Towards the end of cooking add chilli flakes.

2 Force mixture through a sieve, or process in a mouli. If using a blender or processor, go easy as the ideal texture is coarse with little pieces of zucchini visible. Season with salt to taste before serving.

SERVES 4 TO 6

≈ **POTATO, ONION AND ZUCCHINI SOUP**
Based on licurdia, a soup from Cosenza in Calabria, this version is simple, flavoursome and attractive. It makes a good first course before a roast or lasagne, and is equally delicious when served lightly chilled on a hot summer's day.

2 tablespoons brandy

freshly ground black pepper

1 TO PREPARE POLENTA: Bring water to the boil in a large heavy-based saucepan. Reduce to a simmer, then very gradually pour in polenta, stirring constantly. Keep stirring until the polenta lifts away from the sides of the pan, about 20 minutes. Stir in butter. Turn out into an oiled pan to 1 cm

SAUSAGE AND BEAN SOUP

≈ SAUSAGE AND
BEAN SOUP

*This soup from the
Trentino is hearty but not
stodgy or heavy. Once all
the vegetables have been
prepared it doesn't take
hours to stew, relying on
the crisp fresh flavour
of the green vegetables.
However, it still
reheats well.*

3 tablespoons vegetable oil

3 Brattwurst sausages or other coarse-
fleshed tasty sausage

60 g (2 oz) butter

2 onions, finely chopped

2 cloves garlic, finely chopped

1 large leek, cleaned and sliced

2 carrots, diced

2 large potatoes, diced

2 tablespoons plain (all-purpose) flour

1 tablespoon tomato paste

8 cups (2 litres/64 fl oz) beef stock

100 g (3 oz) green beans, cut into
2 cm (¾ in) lengths

salt and freshly ground black pepper

100 g (3 oz) broad beans

100 g (3 oz) peas

100 g (3 oz) Cabanossi salami, cut into
1 cm(½ in) pieces

2 tablespoons finely chopped fresh parsley

1 Heat ½ tablespoon of the vegetable oil in
a large stock pot and gently fry sausages
until cooked through. Remove and when
cool, cut into 2 cm (¾ in) pieces. Pour off
fatty oil from pot.

2 Add remaining oil and butter to pot and
gently sauté onion and garlic until golden,
about 10 minutes. Add leeks and sauté
1 minute more. Add carrots and potatoes,
toss to combine then stir in flour. Cook,
stirring, until vegetables are well coated.

3 Add tomato paste and stock, bring to the
boil, then add beans and season with salt and
pepper. Simmer for 10 minutes before
adding broad beans and peas. Simmer a
further 5 minutes then add Brattwurst,
Cabanossi and parsley and heat for a few
minutes more. Season to taste before serving.

SERVES 6 TO 8

ZUPPA DI COZZE

1 kg (2 lb) fresh mussels

handful plain flour

2 tablespoons olive oil

40 g (1½ oz) butter

1 leek, white part only, finely chopped

3 cloves garlic, minced

pinch saffron flakes or powder

1 tablespoon finely chopped coriander
or parsley

1 small red chilli, minced

⅔ cup (150 ml/5 fl oz) dry white wine

200 g (6½ oz) fresh tomatoes, peeled, seeded and chopped

1 cup (250 ml/8 fl oz) water

salt

1 Put mussels in a bowl, sprinkle with flour and cover with cold water. Leave for 15 minutes then drain, scrub and debeard them, discarding any which are open.

2 Heat oil and butter in a large saucepan and sauté leek and garlic over a low heat until leeks are softened but not brown. Add saffron, coriander and chilli and cook, stirring, 1 to 2 minutes. Increase heat and add wine. Bring to the boil and bubble for 1 to 2 minutes, then add tomatoes and water. Simmer with the lid on for 20 minutes. Check consistency here; it may be neccessary to increase heat and boil to thicken slightly.

3 Add mussels to pan and cook, covered, until they are opened. Discard any which are now unopened, and throw away the shells of one-third of the remaining so that the soup is not crowded with shells. Season to taste. Serve immediately with crusty bread.

SERVES 6

Zuppa di Cozze

≈ MUSSEL SOUP

Mussels seem to be at their best in soup. In Zuppa di Cozze they contrast well with the subtle flavour of the broth and there is great eye appeal as well.

SPLIT PEA AND PUMPKIN SOUP

30 g (1 oz) butter

1 tablespoon olive oil

1 onion, finely chopped

1 ½ cups (250 g/7 oz) yellow split peas

350 g (11 oz) peeled and seeded pumpkin, cut into small pieces

6 cups (1 ½ litres/48 fl oz) chicken stock

salt and white pepper

pinch nutmeg

4 teaspoons pesto (optional, see Coriander Pesto page 35)

≈ **SPLIT PEA AND PUMPKIN SOUP**

The texture of this soup is thick and rustic. If a smoother consistency is preferred, before continuing through step 2 transfer to a blender and purée.

Leftover mashed pumpkin or potato, even cauliflower, can be used in most instances to thicken and flavour sauces or soups.

1 Heat butter and oil in a large saucepan. Add onion and gently fry over a low heat until soft. Stir in split peas then add pumpkin and half the chicken stock. Season with salt, pepper and nutmeg. Bring to the boil and simmer, uncovered, until the peas are tender and the pumpkin is disintegrating. If neccessary, top up with more of the stock as it is cooking.

2 Add remaining stock, adjust seasoning and spoon into warmed bowls. Swirl a teaspoon of pesto through each before serving.

SERVES 4 TO 6

BORLOTTI BEAN DIP

Reminiscent of the Arab hummus, this spread is based on La Capriata, the broad bean purée found in various forms in all the southern regions. Any type of dried bean can be substituted, and if dried broad beans can be found, all the better. Use 185 g (6 oz) dried beans if starting from scratch.

1 clove garlic

1 tablespoon fresh rosemary leaves

400 g (13 oz) canned borlotti beans, drained and rinsed

1 teaspoon tomato paste

½ teaspoon salt

2 tablespoons fresh lemon juice

3 tablespoons extra virgin olive oil

chilli paste or sauce, to taste

extra rosemary sprigs, to garnish

1 Finely chop garlic and rosemary together. Blend in a food processor or mince finely with a fork with beans, tomato paste and salt until a smooth purée forms.

2 Add lemon juice, olive oil and a little chilli paste. Process to blend, then taste. Add more chilli if preferred.

3 Refrigerate, covered, until ready to use; this is even better if left for 24 hours.

Serve as a dip, or on triangles of plain toast topped with a sprig of rosemary.

SERVES 4

ONION FOCACCIA

Using a dough which is yeastless but with a good flavour and texture, this focaccia is quick and easy. The filling, which can be made in advance and stored in the refrigerator, can also be used to stuff a bought plain focaccia.

DOUGH

4 cups (500 g/1 lb) plain (all-purpose) flour, sifted

3 tablespoons caster sugar

½ teaspoon salt

2 eggs, lightly beaten

¾ cup (180 ml/6 fl oz) olive oil

⅓ cup (100 ml/3 fl oz) dry white wine

FILLING

3 tablespoons olive oil

850 g (1¾ lb) onions, sliced and then chopped

3 tablespoons dry white wine

salt and freshly ground black pepper

2¾ cups (700 ml/23 fl oz) water

6 black olives, pitted and sliced

2 teaspoons tiny capers

FOR THE TOP

olive oil

coarse sea salt

cayenne pepper

1 TO PREPARE DOUGH: Mix flour, sugar and salt in a bowl. Gradually incorporate eggs, oil and wine, beating well after each addition. A little more wine or flour may be needed to form a loose dough. Transfer to a floured board and knead 2 to 3 minutes, or until smooth. (This whole step can be done in a food processor.) Cover and refrigerate for at least 30 minutes.

2 Preheat oven to 200°C (400°F). Grease a large rectangular scone tray and toss it with flour.

3 TO PREPARE FILLING: Heat oil in a large, heavy saucepan. Add onions and wine, and salt and pepper well. Simmer, uncovered, for 5 minutes, stirring from time to time. Add water. Simmer until all the liquid has evaporated; the mixture must be quite dry. Stir in olives and capers.

4 Roll out dough on a lightly floured board to a rectangle about 1 cm (½ in) thick. Spread filling over one end to cover half, leaving a rim of 2 to 3 cm (1 in) free. Fold over other half to encase, and lightly press edges together. Transfer to prepared tray, drizzle over 1 to 2 tablespoons of olive oil and sprinkle with salt and cayenne. Dimple surface using fingertips.

5 Transfer to the oven and bake until golden and cooked through, 20 to 25 minutes. Cool slightly before removing from tray. Can be served warm or at room temperature.

SERVES 4 TO 6

Onion Focaccia

FARFALLE WITH BACON AND PEPPERCORNS

30 g (1 oz) butter

90 g (3 oz) lean bacon, cut into very thin strips

1 spring onion, sliced

¾ cup (180 ml/6 fl oz) cream

salt

1½ tablespoons pink peppercorns

1½ tablespoons green peppercorns

2 egg yolks, lightly beaten

275 g (9 oz) farfalle

1 Heat butter in a large pan and sauté bacon until crisp. Add spring onion and half the cream and bring to the boil. Taste for salt and stir in peppercorns. Cook gently until slightly thickened, then reduce heat and keep warm.

2 Whip remaining cream until thick, then stir in egg yolks. Gently stir into sauce, bring to the boil and taste for salt.

3 In the meantime, cook farfalle in plenty of boiling salted water until *al dente*. Drain and add to sauce in pan. Toss quickly to coat and serve at once.

SERVES 4

≈ **VERSATILE CARROTS**

These marinated carrot sticks make a good addition to an antipasti spread giving colour, texture and a touch of chilli. They are also good served with a barbecue or taken on a picnic as they are ideal finger food. More or less chilli may be used, and other herbs can be substituted for the basil. Carrots treated this way last for weeks if kept covered in the refrigerator.

MARINATED CARROTS

1½ teaspoons salt

8 carrots, cut into sticks

2 tablespoons olive oil

3 cloves garlic, cut into halves

¼ teaspoon chilli flakes

1 tablespoon finely chopped fresh basil

white wine vinegar

1 Bring a large saucepan of water to the boil, add 1 teaspoon salt and carrot sticks. Boil until just cooked but still crisp, 3 to 4 minutes. Drain and cool slightly before transferring to a bowl.

2 Add remaining ½ teaspoon salt, olive oil, garlic, chilli flakes and basil. Add enough vinegar to just cover carrots then toss to distribute ingredients.

3 Cover, and refrigerate for at least 24 hours before use. Drain before serving.

SERVES 4

TAGLIERINI WITH SALMON, PEAS AND LEMON

250 g (8 oz) shelled young peas

salt

400 g (13 oz) fresh taglierini or 250 g (8 oz) dried

90 g (3 oz) butter

1 tablespoon vegetable oil

1 clove garlic

350 g (11 oz) fresh salmon, skinned, boned and cut into 2 cm (¾ in) cubes

3 tablespoons finely chopped fresh parsley

freshly ground black pepper

¼ teaspoon grated lemon zest

1 teaspoon fresh lemon juice

1 Bring a large saucepan of water to the boil, add peas and a pinch of salt and simmer until *al dente*. Scoop from water and reserve. Add pasta to the pot and cook until *al dente*.

2 In the meantime, heat butter and oil in a frying pan and briefly sauté clove garlic. Add salmon with a pinch of salt and sauté gently until opaque, but not browned. Add peas and parsley to pan and cook, stirring, for 1 minute. Discard garlic. Season with pepper and stir in lemon zest and juice.

3 When pasta is ready, drain and add to sauce. Toss lightly to coat and serve at once. It is not usual to serve cheese with this sauce.

SERVES 4

Taglierini with Salmon, Peas and Lemon

*Roasted Asparagus
with Fontina*

≈ FONTINA

*Fontina is the famous
melting cheese from
Piedmont which goes into
fonduta, the creamy
Italian version of fondue.
Used in a sauce for
asparagus it makes an
elegant but rich first
course. It is not neccessary
to use imported Italian
Fontina as that made
elsewhere will be just as
successful here.*

ROASTED ASPARAGUS WITH FONTINA

**225 g (7 oz) Fontina cheese, cut into
small dice**

milk

30 g (1 oz) butter

2 egg yolks, beaten

salt and white pepper

**1 kg (2 lb) fresh asparagus, trimmed
and peeled**

2 tablespoons olive oil

Parmesan cheese, grated

1 Put Fontina in a bowl and pour in enough milk to just cover. Set aside for at least 4 hours to allow the cheese to absorb the milk.

2 Preheat oven to 260°C (500°F).

3 Gently melt butter in the top of a double saucepan. Maintain a hot temperature, but do not allow water to boil. Add the cheese and any remaining milk, and stir in the egg yolks. Cook gently, stirring, until the mixture is thick and creamy. Season with salt and pepper and keep warm.

4 Place asparagus on a baking tray and pour over the olive oil. Toss with your fingers to coat them well, then space them over the tray so that they don't touch. Place in the oven and roast for 7 to 10 minutes, depending on thickness.

5 Arrange asparagus on warmed plates and spoon the fonduta over the top. Serve at once with grated Parmesan cheese.

SERVES 4 TO 6

AVOCADO WITH ANCHOVY AND LEMON DRESSING

3 anchovy fillets in oil

milk

1 tablespoon finely minced or grated onion

1 teaspoon smooth mild mustard

3 tablespoons extra virgin olive oil

1 tablespoon white wine vinegar

2 teaspoons fresh lemon juice

½ teaspoon grated lemon zest

white pepper

2 avocados, halved, peeled and seeded

1 lemon cut into wedges

1 Drain anchovies, cover with a little milk and soak for 30 minutes. Pour off excess milk and mince with a fork. Transfer to a bowl with the onion, mustard, olive oil, vinegar, lemon juice and zest. Combine well and season with pepper.

2 Cut each avocado half into 6 to 8 slices along its length and arrange on a plate. Dress with sauce and serve, garnished with lemon wedges.

SERVES 4

GARLIC AND PARMESAN GRISSINI

3 cups (375 g/12 oz) plain (all-purpose) flour

1 tablespoon baking powder

1 teaspoon salt

1 cup (125 g/4 oz) grated Parmesan cheese

125 g (4 oz) butter, melted and cooled

1 large egg, beaten

3 cloves garlic, minced

½ cup (125 ml/4 fl oz) lukewarm water

sesame or poppy seeds (optional)

butter and flour for baking tray

1 Preheat oven to 190°C (375°F).

2 This step may be done in a processor. Sift the flour, baking powder and salt into a bowl, then stir in Parmesan. Make a well in the centre and add butter, egg, garlic and water. Stir until just mixed, then turn out onto a board and knead lightly for 5 minutes incorporating more flour if neccessary to keep dough dry. Cover and refrigerate 30 minutes.

3 On a floured surface, roll out dough evenly to a rectangle about 25 x 30 cm (10 x 12 in) and ¾ cm (½ in) thick. Using a pastry wheel or long knife, cut into strips ¾ cm (½ in) wide, and of desired length. If using sesame or poppy seeds, lightly roll bread sticks in these.

4 Butter and flour a baking tray, then arrange breadsticks 2 cm (¾ in) apart. Bake for 15 to 20 minutes, or until golden. For a softer dough, reduce oven temperature to 170°C (340°F) after the first 5 minutes.

MAKES ABOUT 50 x 12 CM (5 IN) STICKS

DEEP-FRIED RAVIOLI

vegetable oil for deep frying

500 g (1 lb) ravioli, uncooked

salt

1 In a large saucepan or deep-fryer, heat enough oil to give a depth of at least 5 cm (2 in). When a piece of bread begins to bubble as soon as it is put in, the oil is hot enough (180°C (350°F) on a thermometer).

2 Begin to fry the ravioli in batches and cook until they turn golden and start to blister. As they are done, transfer with a slotted spoon to paper towels. Sprinkle with salt to taste while they are still hot. Serve at once, accompanied by a dipping sauce (and cocktail sticks) if desired.

SERVES 6 TO 8

≈ **STORING GRISSINI**

When stored in an airtight jar, these breadsticks keep crisp for weeks. They may be baked for less time to give a softer, more breadlike texture; in which case they don't keep as well. They can be cut into short lengths to be served as snacks, or longer sticks to serve at table.

≈ **DEEP-FRIED RAVIOLI**

Served either plain or with a dipping sauce, here's a change from the usual nibbles to have with drinks. Frozen, fresh or dried ravioli can be used, and those with a spicy meat filling work very well.

The word 'calzone' is Italian slang for trousers, and it is used to describe a folded pizza. If you can envisage the old-fashioned buttoned breeches being wrapped around legs, it is easy to see where the story arose. One story about how the calzone developed is based on the fact that, if a pizza is folded in half, it only takes up half as much room in the oven and so, doubles production!

CHICKEN CALZONE

This calzone is a breeze, as leftover chicken or turkey meat can be used and the pastry is yeastless, which eliminates the time needed for the dough to rise. Smaller, individual calzoni can also be made with this recipe; to get 7 or 8, cut rolled dough into 12 cm (5 in) diameter circles.

PASTRY

1 ¼ cups (155 g/5 oz) plain (all-purpose) flour

large pinch salt

125 g (4 oz) butter, at room temperature, cut into pieces

2 large eggs

4 tablespoons white wine

FILLING

100 g (3 ½ oz) cooked chicken meat, diced

60 g (2 oz) lean bacon, diced

100 g (3 ½ oz) mozzarella cheese (preferably fresh), diced

250 g (8 oz) ricotta cheese

1 tablespoon chopped spring onion

2 eggs, lightly beaten

2 tablespoons grated Parmesan cheese

salt and freshly ground black pepper

1 egg, lightly beaten

1 TO PREPARE PASTRY: Mix flour and salt, then cut butter through with a fork until a breadcrumb-like texture forms. Work in eggs, one at a time, and then add wine gradually until a dry but pliable dough forms. Knead until smooth. Cover with a damp cloth or plastic wrap and chill for 1 hour.

(This step can be done in a food processor.)

2 Preheat oven to 200°C (400°F).

3 TO PREPARE FILLING: Put all ingredients except salt, pepper and egg in a bowl and combine well. Season to taste with salt and pepper.

4 Roll out dough on a floured surface to a circle 30 cm (12 in) diameter. Place the filling over half the circle, leaving a 2 cm (¾ in) rim free around the edge. Paint this edge with some of the beaten egg. Fold the other half of the dough over filling and seal the two sides together. Fold the edges over and in on themselves, and pinch them together to form a pattern. Paint the surface with remaining egg.

5 Transfer calzone to a greased baking tray and put in the oven for 25 to 30 minutes, or until pastry is golden. Allow to cool for a few minutes before serving.

SERVES 4 TO 5

BAKED WHOLE EGGPLANT

4 small young eggplant (aubergine)

4 cloves garlic, cut into slivers

extra virgin olive oil

salt and freshly ground black pepper

1 lemon, quartered

1 Preheat oven to 200°C (400°F).

2 Pierce each eggplant 6 to 8 times all over its surface, and insert a sliver of garlic into each slit.

3 Transfer to the oven and space over the wire racks. Bake for about 20 minutes, or until the skins are wrinkled and the flesh is soft when pressed.

4 Remove from oven and cool for a few minutes. With a sharp or serrated knife, remove stalks and slice each eggplant along its length into even slices 1 to 2 cm (½ in) thick.

Arrange in a fan-like pattern on plates, dress with olive oil, salt and pepper and serve with a wedge of lemon each. Serve at once, or cool to room temperature.

SERVES 4 AS A STARTER, OR 8 TO 10 AS PART OF AN ANTIPASTI

LINGUINE WITH BEETROOT

250 g (8 oz) beetroot, cooked and trimmed

40 g (1 ½ oz) butter

1 tablespoon finely chopped onion

2 sprigs fresh thyme

salt and freshly ground black pepper

3 tablespoons dry white wine

⅔ cup (150 ml/5 fl oz) cream

2 egg yolks, lightly beaten

350 g (11 oz) fresh linguine or 250 g (8 oz) dried

1 Cut one-third of the beetroot into julienne strips and reserve for garnish. Cut the remaining two-thirds into larger pieces.

2 Heat butter in a large pan and add pieces of beetroot, onion and 1 sprig thyme. Sauté gently 2 to 3 minutes, season lightly with salt and pepper and pour in wine. Cook, stirring, over a high heat to reduce wine. When the mixture is almost dry, transfer to a blender or processor and blend until smooth. Return to pan and keep warm.

3 Whip cream until thick, then stir in egg yolks. Gradually add to beetroot in pan and bring to the boil, stirring. Taste for salt and pepper.

4 In the meantime, cook pasta in plenty of boiling salted water until *al dente*. Drain, add to sauce and toss to coat well. Transfer to warmed pasta bowls, decorate with reserved beetroot and sprinkle over remaining thyme leaves. Serve accompanied by any grated cheese.

SERVES 4

Linguine with Beetroot

SFOGLIATINE

Sfogliatine ripiene (literally, stuffed pastries) are small, filled pastries made on flaky or puff pastry. The original come from Liguria and have a cheese and spinach stuffing, but many different fillings are successful, such as the tomato, olive and mozzarella used here. Sfogliatine can be made smaller and served as finger food to nibble on with drinks.

1 large tomato

125 g (4 oz) fresh mozzarella, cut into very small cubes

¼ teaspoon finely chopped fresh basil

¼ teaspoon finely chopped fresh oregano, or pinch dried

8 to 10 black olives, pitted and sliced

salt and freshly ground black pepper

220 g (7 oz) puff pastry

1 large egg, beaten

1 Preheat oven to 190°C (375°F).

2 Dip tomato into boiling water for a few seconds, then peel, seed and chop into very small cubes. Combine with mozzarella, basil, oregano and olives, then season with salt and pepper.

3 On a floured surface, roll out pastry to 2 to 3 mm (⅛ in) thickness. Cut out circles of 10 cm (4 in) diameter, and paint around the rims of each with egg. Place some filling on one half of each circle, fold over the other side to encase it, and press tightly to seal. Trim around the outer edges with a crinkle-cutter, or press with the tines of a fork. Brush the tops with remaining egg, and transfer to an ungreased baking tray.

4 Bake for 15 to 20 minutes, or until golden and puffed. Serve hot or cold as a snack.

MAKES ABOUT 15, OR 24 SMALLER VERSIONS FOR FINGER FOOD

---

extra cup or two of Bolognese sauce that didn't get used, or the tail end of a salami and those pieces of cheese always lurking in your refrigerator!

SPINACH FETTUCCINE WITH TOASTED FLOUR SAUCE

185 g (6 oz) butter

2 onions, finely chopped

2 tablespoons plain (all-purpose) flour

5 tablespoons grated Parmesan cheese

freshly ground black pepper

400 g (13 oz) fresh spinach fettuccine, or 250 g (8 oz) dried

1 Preheat oven to 170°C (325°F).

2 Melt butter in a pan and add onion. Stir to coat, cover, and cook over a low heat until soft and golden, 25 to 30 minutes. Do not brown.

3 Spread flour in a small baking or pie dish and toast in the oven until brown, about 20 minutes. Cool, then stir through Parmesan and a few good grinds of pepper.

4 In the meantime, cook the pasta in boiling salted water until al dente. Drain and transfer to warmed serving plates. Sprinkle with the flour mixture and toss through butter and onion. Serve at once.

SERVES 4

FRESH FIGS WITH PROSCIUTTO

3 tablespoons freshly grated Parmesan cheese

1 tablespoon finely grated lemon zest

125 g (4 oz) butter

4 thin slices prosciutto, cut in half

8 fresh, ripe figs

1 Combine Parmesan and lemon zest and set aside.

2 Melt butter in a saucepan and bring to bubbling over a moderate heat. Continue simmering until it clarifies (the fats separate) and the colour turns golden brown. Strain, and keep warm.

3 Wrap a strip of prosciutto around the middle of each fig. Place on a rack well

ALESSI BOWL FROM VENTURA IMPORTS

below a hot grill and heat through, about 2 minutes. Arrange 2 per serve on warmed plates, spoon over some browned butter and sprinkle some of the Parmesan mix on top. Serve immediately, accompanied by the rest of the Parmesan mix.

SERVES 4

PAPPA COL POMODORO

5 tablespoons extra virgin olive oil

90 g (3 oz) white onion, chopped

2 large cloves garlic, minced

800 g (1 lb 10 oz) firm ripe tomatoes, chopped (only peel if you will be using a processor instead of a mouli)

5 to 6 fresh basil leaves

5 cups (1 ¼ litres/40 fl oz) light chicken or vegetable stock

200 g (6 ½ oz) thickly sliced white country-style bread

salt and freshly ground black pepper

2 additional tablespoons extra virgin olive oil

1 Heat oil in a large pan and lightly sauté onion and garlic until softened. Add tomatoes and basil and simmer over a low heat for 15 minutes. Remove from heat, cool slightly then pass through a mouli or coarsely purée in a processor.

2 In the meantime, heat the stock in a large saucepan.

3 Toast bread on both sides under a grill, then transfer to the saucepan. Add tomato purée and salt and pepper to taste. Simmer, uncovered, until the bread breaks down and a smooth, dense texture results. Taste for salt, give a few good grinds of pepper and stir in the extra oil.

SERVES 4

Fresh Figs with Prosciutto

≈ PAPPA COL POMODORO

No, this doesn't refer to the father of all tomatoes, but to a soup based on bread with, in this case, tomatoes. A legacy of Tuscan cooking, Pappa col Pomodoro relies on few but good ingredients and canned tomatoes can't be successfully substituted. It can be served hot, at room temperature or chilled.

LIGHT MEALS

Pasta ... its form, ingredients and uses vary greatly throughout Italy. For instance, unique to Abruzzi, a mountainous region on the Adriatic coast, is the *chitarra*, a wooden frame roughly in the shape of a guitar, strung on each side with wire. Pasta dough is rolled over the wire, which cuts it into strips similar to linguine.

Pasta from Abruzzi has an excellent reputation, said to be because of the quality of the local water used in the making. A good number of the pasta shapes common today began in Apulia, which has bumper crops of durum wheat. Apulians are Italy's prima pasta eaters, but due to the lack of eggs in the region in the past, their homemade pasta today is often still egg-less.

Because pasta is widely eaten the Italians have evolved a myriad of sauces, many now world-famed, such as the redoubtable pesto. There's even a tomato and onion sauce that uses stones from the seabed to add a seafood flavour! Often originated for pasta, this endlessly diverse variety of sauces is just as likely to be used today to dress vegetables or be tossed through stir-fried meats.

Torta Pasquale (page 33); Pappardelle with Sun-dried Tomatoes (page 37); Spaghetti and Prawns (page 34)

PENNE MARE E MONTE

SAUCE

40 g (1½ oz) butter

¼ cup (30 g/1½ oz) plain (all-purpose) flour

2 cups (500 ml/16 fl oz) milk

1 bay leaf

pinch nutmeg

salt and freshly ground black pepper

1 tablespoon fresh lemon juice

500 g (1 lb) penne

4 tablespoons extra virgin olive oil

2 leeks, trimmed and thinly sliced

1 thin zucchini (courgette), julienned

500 g (1 lb) button mushrooms, sliced

½ cup (125 ml/4 fl oz) dry white wine

salt and freshly ground black pepper

300 g (10 oz) canned tuna in oil, drained

1 Preheat oven to 200°C (400°F). Grease a shallow-sided ovenproof dish.

2 TO PREPARE SAUCE: Melt butter in a saucepan and stir in flour. Cook until bubbling then gradually stir in milk. Add bay leaf and cook over a moderate heat, stirring often, until thickened. Season with nutmeg, salt and pepper and stir in lemon juice. Remove from heat and set aside.

3 Cook penne in plenty of boiling salted water until *al dente*. Drain and stir through 1 tablespoon of the oil.

4 Heat remaining oil in a pan and gently sauté leeks until softened. Add zucchini and mushrooms, sauté 1 minute then add wine. Cook over high heat for 10 to 15 seconds then season to taste with salt and pepper and sauté 1 minute. Remove bay leaf from sauce and then add three-quarters of sauce and the penne to pan. Toss to combine and transfer to prepared dish.

5 Break the tuna up and distribute throughout the penne. Spoon over remaining sauce. Transfer to oven and bake until hot, about 20 minutes. Serve at once.

SERVES 6

POLENTA PASTICCIATA

SAUCE

40 g (1½ oz) butter

2 tablespoons plain (all-purpose) flour

1¾ cups (420 ml/14 fl oz) milk

salt and white pepper

pinch nutmeg

90 g (3 oz) grated cheese, such as Cheddar, Emmenthal or Fontina

4 cups (1 litre/32 fl oz) water

½ teaspoon salt

220 g (7 oz) polenta

100 g (3½ oz) butter, cut into pieces

300 g (10 oz) button mushrooms, sliced

salt and freshly ground black pepper

pinch nutmeg

480 g (15 oz) drained artichoke hearts, sliced

3 tomatoes, sliced

180 g (6 oz) double smoked ham, thinly sliced

2 tablespoons grated Parmesan cheese

1 Preheat oven to 200°C (400°F). Oil an ovenproof dish.

2 TO PREPARE SAUCE: Melt butter in a saucepan and stir in flour. Cook briefly, then gradually blend in milk. Stir until thickened. Season with salt and pepper to taste, and nutmeg. Add cheese. Cook, stirring, until sauce is smooth.

3 Boil water in a large saucepan. Add salt and gradually stir in polenta. Reduce heat and cook, stirring often, for 20 minutes. Remove from heat and stir in half the butter.

4 Meanwhile, melt remaining butter and gently sauté mushrooms for 3 to 4 minutes. Season with salt, pepper and nutmeg.

5 Spread one-third of polenta into prepared dish and top with one-third mushrooms. Then one-third artichoke hearts, one-third tomato slices, one-third ham, and one-third sauce. Repeat these layers twice. Sprinkle with Parmesan and bake for 30 minutes. Stand for 3 to 4 minutes before serving.

SERVES 4

Penne Mare e Monte (front); Polenta Pasticciata (back)

≈ PENNE OF THE SEA AND THE MOUNTAINS

Penne Mare e Monte — an appealing baked pasta dish using tuna (from the sea) and mushrooms (from the mountains), this can be prepared in advance and popped in the oven just before serving.

Use imported tuna from Italy if possible

≈ POLENTA PASTICCIATA

Sometimes callea Pastissada, this is a pie of filled and baked polenta which can be found all over northern Italy in one version or another. Every town, every cook has their special recipe which is of course supremo, but this one is hard to beat.

GLASS BOWL FROM CYDONIA THE GLASS STUDIO. PLATE FROM VILLEROY & BOCH. CUTLERY FROM BIBELOT

ASPARAGUS FRITTATA

6 eggs

¼ cup (60 ml/2 fl oz) cream

1 tablespoon plain (all-purpose) flour

pinch nutmeg

3 tablespoons grated Parmesan cheese

salt and white pepper

400 g (13 oz) cooked green asparagus spears, either canned or fresh

1 tablespoon finely diced spring onion

2 tablespoons olive oil

1 In a bowl whisk eggs, cream, flour, nutmeg, Parmesan, and salt and pepper to taste.

2 Cut half the asparagus spears into 2 cm (¾ in) lengths and add to custard along with the spring onion.

3 Heat oil in a large heavy-based frying pan. Add custard and arrange remaining asparagus spears in a spoke-like pattern around the surface. Cover pan, turn heat down to very low and cook until the frittata is set, about 20 minutes. Serve warm.

SERVES 6 TO 8

TUNA AND WHITE BEAN SALAD

1 clove garlic, minced

1 teaspoon finely chopped fresh thyme, or ¼ teaspoon dried

1 tablespoon finely chopped fresh parsley

3 tablespoons white wine vinegar

4 tablespoons extra virgin olive oil

salt and freshly ground black pepper

600 g (1 lb 3 oz) cooked cannellini beans

1 large red onion, coarsely chopped

750 g (1 ½ lb) canned tuna in oil, drained and broken up into chunks

3 hard-boiled eggs, sliced into wedges

3 tomatoes, sliced into wedges

1 Combine garlic, thyme, parsley, vinegar and olive oil and mix with a fork until blended. Season with salt and pepper.

2 Place beans and onion into a large bowl, add dressing and toss to coat well. Add tuna, toss gently, then add half the egg wedges and half the tomato. Lightly combine. Serve piled onto a platter with the remaining egg and tomato wedges for garnish.

SERVES 4 TO 6

BACKGROUND FROM TERAZZO & CO PTY LTD, WHITE BOWL FROM CYDONIA THE GLASS STUDIO

≈ CANNELLINI BEANS

Using canned ready cooked cannellini beans is convenient, but as with all dried beans, boiling them yourself gives a better texture and is more economical. Remember, dried beans which are old don't cook properly.

Cover beans well with cold water and leave to soak overnight in a warm spot. This step is necessary to prevent the skins from splitting. Then drain them, cover with fresh cold water and bring to the boil. Simmer for 2 hours, only salting at the end.

Asparagus Frittata, Tuna and White Bean Salad

HAZELNUT AND RICOTTA AGNOLOTTI

PASTA

3¼ cups (400 g/13 oz) plain (all-purpose) flour

large pinch salt

4 eggs

FILLING

⅔ cup (100 g/3½ oz) roasted and peeled hazelnuts (filberts)

100 g (3½ oz) ricotta cheese

½ cup (60 g/2 oz) grated Parmesan cheese

yolk of 1 large egg

good pinch nutmeg

pinch salt

1 to 2 tablespoons milk

1 egg white, beaten

SAUCE

90 g (3 oz) butter

4 tablespoons cream

5 to 6 small fresh sage leaves

2 tablespoons freshly grated Parmesan cheese

1 TO PREPARE PASTA: Pile flour on a work surface, make a well in the centre and add salt and eggs. Using a fork, break up eggs and begin to incorporate the flour. Continue blending until you have a loosely formed

Hazelnut and Ricotta Agnolotti

mass of dough. The dough may be made in a processor up to this point.

Begin kneading by hand, adding a little more flour or water as needed. Continue kneading until a smooth elastic ball is formed. Cover with a damp cloth or plastic wrap and rest for 30 minutes. Divide the ball into four, then using a rolling pin or a hand-cranked pasta machine, roll out each in turn to a very thin, even sheet. Rest, covered.

2 TO PREPARE FILLING: Crush hazelnuts in a mortar or use a rolling pin over a hard surface. Avoid processing, as this tends to purée the nuts. In a bowl combine them with ricotta, Parmesan, nutmeg and salt. Stir in just enough milk to form a paste.

3 Using a cookie cutter or an upturned glass, cut out circles from the sheets of pasta about 5 cm (2 in) in diameter. Keep all the pasta covered as you work to avoid drying out. Working a few at a time, paint around the rim of each circle with egg white. Place a little of the filling in the centre of each, then fold it over to form a half moon shape. Firmly press the edges together then cut around them with a zig-zag pastry wheel. As the agnolotti are formed, place them in a single layer and dust very lightly with flour.

4 When they are all made, simmer in boiling salted water until *al dente*, 3 to 4 minutes.

5 TO PREPARE SAUCE: Melt butter in a saucepan and cook over a low heat until browned. Strain into another pan and add cream and sage. Heat gently to thicken slightly, then stir in Parmesan. Keep warm.

5 Drain agnolotti, transfer to a warmed serving dish and toss through the sauce. Serve at once, accompanied with extra grated Parmesan.

SERVES 4

TORTA PASQUALE

Savoury Easter pies are common to most of Italy, and although there are many variations they are all meatless or di magro, literally meaning lean.

500 g (1 lb) puff pastry

750 g (1 ½ lb) pre-cooked spinach, squeezed dry and chopped

large pinch nutmeg

¼ teaspoon salt

2 tablespoons grated Parmesan cheese

freshly ground black pepper

2 eggs, beaten

300 g (10 oz) artichoke hearts, sliced into 5 along their lengths

3 hard-boiled eggs, each cut into 5 to 6 slices

2 tablespoons pine nuts

1 Preheat oven to 200°C (400°F) and grease a 21 cm (8 in) springform pan.

2 Divide puff pastry in two, roughly two-thirds and one-third of whole. Roll out the larger piece, then line prepared pan, bringing it 5 to 6 cm (about 2 in) up the sides.

3 In a bowl mix spinach, nutmeg, salt, Parmesan and pepper to taste. Add three-quarters of the beaten eggs and combine well. Reserve remaining egg for glazing.

4 Layer one-third of the spinach in pie base and cover with the artichoke slices in a single layer. Put another one-third of spinach on this, then cover with the egg slices. Layer the remaining spinach on top.

5 Roll out remaining pastry and place over the pie. Press top and bottom edges tightly and pinch the two together. Trim edges before painting the surface with reserved egg. Make one or two small cuts in the pastry, then sprinkle the pine nuts on top. Place in the oven and bake until pastry is golden, about 45 minutes. Allow to cool slighty before removing from pan. Can be served warm or cold.

SERVES 4 TO 6

≈ **TORTA PASQUALE**
In Liguria where this recipe is from, spinach is frequently used and spring artichokes are in good supply. In other regions a Torta Pasquale will often contain ricotta but this cheese was not commonly used in traditional Ligurian kitchens until quite recently. Whole or sliced eggs are baked into the pie and this signifies the ever regenerating elements of nature after the passing of winter.

ONION TART

vegetable oil

100 g (3½ oz) bacon, trimmed and diced

3 cloves garlic

8 to 10 thick slices white bread, crusts removed

40 g (½ oz) butter

900 g (1 lb 13 oz) onions, sliced then roughly chopped

salt

2 tablespoons fresh parsley, finely chopped

8 eggs

1½ cups (375 ml/12 fl oz) milk

3 tablespoons plain (all-purpose) flour

¼ teaspoon white pepper

¼ teaspoon nutmeg

1 Preheat oven to 180°C (350°F).

2 Heat 1 tablespoon of vegetable oil in a large frying pan and cook bacon pieces, stirring, for 2 to 3 minutes. Do not crisp. Drain on absorbent towels and set aside. Add more oil and the garlic to pan and, when heated, toast bread slices on each side until golden. Set aside.

3 Add more oil to pan to make up to 2 tablespoons and add butter. When bubbling remove garlic and add onions, a sprinkling of salt and half the parsley. Cook gently, stirring often, until onions are soft and golden, about 30 minutes. If neccessary, add a little water from time to time to keep onions moist.

4 Meanwhile, grease a large rectangular pie dish with oil and line it with the toast.

5 Mix eggs, milk, flour, pepper and nutmeg in a bowl to form a smooth batter. When onions are ready, stir them through batter evenly. Gently pour mixture over toast crust in the pie dish. It doesn't matter if some of the toast floats up. Sprinkle the bacon and remaining parsley on top and bake until set, 30 to 45 minutes. Let cool slightly before serving.

SERVES 6 TO 8

This is a combination of two dishes: a delicate prawn pasta from the Ligurian coast and a creamy lemon sauce flavoured with grappa from the mountains beyond. If grappa is unavailable or too powerful for you, vodka is a milder substitute.

≈ PERFECTLY EASY PIE

Torta suzanna can be knocked up in a matter of minutes at the mere mention of a festa! It is just as good served cold or warm, and it easily cuts into manageable slices for a buffet or picnic.

SPAGHETTI AND PRAWNS IN LEMON SAUCE

500 g (1 lb) fresh spaghetti, or 300 g (10 oz) dried

1 cup (250 ml/8 fl oz) cream

½ teaspoon grated lemon zest

3 tablespoons grappa

1 tablespoon fresh lemon juice

pinch nutmeg

450 g (14 oz) cooked and peeled prawns (shrimps)

1 Put spaghetti on to boil in a large pot of boiling, salted water. Just before it becomes al dente, drain.

2 Meanwhile, put cream and lemon zest in a frying pan and simmer over a low heat for 5 minutes. Add grappa, lemon juice and nutmeg, cook 1 to 2 minutes, then stir in prawns. Add drained spaghetti, increase heat and cook, stirring, so that the sauce thickens and becomes absorbed by the pasta. Serve at once without cheese.

SERVES 4

TORTA SUZANNA

20 g (⅔ oz) butter or margarine, softened

500 g (1 lb) puff pastry, rolled out to 2 to 3 cm (1½ in)

250 g (8 oz) lean bacon, proscuitto or ham, trimmed

1 tomato, sliced

6 to 8 eggs

freshly ground black pepper

1 tablespoon fresh basil, shredded

beaten egg

1 Preheat oven to 180°C (350°F).

2 Grease a rectangular ovenproof dish with butter or margarine and line with pastry, going up the sides 4 to 5 cm (2 in).

3 Layer bacon across the bottom, then distribute tomato slices over this.

4 Break the eggs over the surface so that the whites run out to meet, and the yolks are roughly equidistant from one another. It doesn't matter if the yolks break. Season with a good sprinkling of pepper and scatter basil over the top.

5 Cover with a layer of pastry, meeting the bottom layer at the sides and sealing them together firmly. Neaten and crimp this edge with your fingers. Paint the surface with beaten egg and prick it with a fork once or twice. Bake, uncovered, until pastry is golden, about 30 minutes. Allow to cool slightly before serving.

SERVES 6 TO 8

CORIANDER PESTO FOR PASTA OR MEAT

This lighter, fresher version of pesto is as good served on pasta as it is tossed through stir-fried chicken or pork. It can also be used to dress vegetables, and it keeps well for days in the refrigerator.

1 large bunch coriander

4 tablespoons pine nuts, lightly toasted

4 tablespoons grated Parmesan cheese

2 cloves garlic, crushed

⅔ cup (150 ml/5 fl oz) light flavoured olive oil

1 Remove stalks from coriander and discard. Combine leaves with pine nuts, Parmesan and garlic and chop finely until a paste-like texture forms, or crush to a paste using a mortar and pestle.

Alternatively, process until almost smooth in a food processor.

2 Slowly add oil. Check the consistency as you may not need all the oil. The sauce is ready when it is smooth and almost runny.

If using a food processor, keep the machine running as you add the oil.

3 Cover and refrigerate, for up to 6 days.

SERVES 4 TO 6

CHICKEN LIVERS WITH PROSCIUTTO AND SAGE

125 g (4 oz) butter

3 tablespoons olive oil

1 clove garlic

8 slices white bread, crusts removed and cut in half diagonally

500 g (1 lb) chicken livers

1 teaspoon fresh sage, finely chopped

salt and freshly ground black pepper

100 g (3½ oz) prosciutto or ham, cut into thin strips

½ cup (125 ml/4 fl oz) dry white wine

40 g (1½ oz) butter, extra

3 to 4 whole sage leaves for garnish

1 Heat half the butter and all the olive oil in a frying pan. Add garlic and sauté bread until golden on both sides. Drain on paper towels and keep warm. Pour off any remaining butter/oil from pan and wipe out with a paper towel.

2 Heat remaining butter in the pan and add chicken livers, sage, and salt and pepper to taste. Quickly sauté livers over a good heat for 2 minutes. Add proscuitto, lower heat and sauté 1 minute more. Remove the livers and proscuitto from pan and transfer to a warm serving plate.

3 Add wine to pan and bring to the boil, scraping up the remains on the bottom of the pan. Boil 1 minute. Add the last 2 tablespoons butter to the sauce, melt and mix, then pour over chicken livers and proscuitto. Serve immediately with the garlic toasts arranged around the plate and topped with whole sage leaves.

SERVES 4

≈ **COATING SAUCES**

When serving coating sauces such as pesto on pasta, it is not neccessary to heat them. Simply stir through 1 to 2 tablespoons of the boiling pasta water just before draining, and your sauce will be warmed and of a good coating consistency.

Lamb and Rosemary Pie

LAMB AND ROSEMARY PIE

≈ PIE PASTRY

The pastry used in this recipe is very versatile and is particularly easy when made in a processor. It can be made into a good pastry for sweet pies with the addition of 2 tablespoons of caster sugar and 1 to 2 teaspoons grated lemon.

PIE PASTRY

2 cups (250 g/8 oz) plain (all-purpose) flour

good pinch salt

100 g (3½ oz) butter, at room temperature, cut into small pieces

1 x 60 g (2 oz) egg

3 to 4 tablespoons cold white wine

FILLING

1 tablespoon vegetable oil

150 g (5 oz) bacon, diced

20 g (⅔ oz) butter

1 onion, chopped

500 g (1 lb) minced lamb

½ teaspoon chopped dried rosemary

salt and freshly ground black pepper

1½ tablespoons plain (all-purpose) flour

½ cup (125 ml/4 fl oz) white wine

¾ cup (200 ml/6 fl oz) water

⅔ cup (150 ml/5 fl oz) cream

2 hard-boiled eggs, each cut into 6 pieces

beaten egg for glaze

1 To Prepare Pastry: Mix flour and salt, then cut butter through with a fork until a breadcrumb-like texture forms. Work in egg, and then add wine gradually until a dry but pliable dough forms. Knead until smooth, then divide into 2 balls, one a bit larger than the other. Cover with a damp cloth or plastic wrap and chill for 1 hour.

(This step can be done in a food processor.)

2 Preheat oven to 200°C (400°F). Grease a 23 cm (9 in) pie dish.

3 To Prepare Filling: Heat oil in a large frying pan and fry bacon until crisp. Remove and set aside. Add butter to pan and when bubbling, add onion. Fry gently until soft, 6 to 8 minutes. Add lamb and sauté until brown. Add rosemary, salt and pepper to taste, and flour. Stir well to coat lamb and to slightly cook flour; 1 to 2 minutes. Stir in wine and cook until evaporated, stirring to deglaze the pan. Stir in water and bring to the boil. Reduce heat and cook, covered, over a gentle heat for 40 minutes. From time to time give it a stir and add more water to maintain a thick gravy. When lamb is tender, remove from heat. Stir through cream and add reserved bacon. Toss through diced egg.

4 TO ASSEMBLE PIE: Take the larger ball of dough and roll out on a floured surface to a 30 cm (12 in) circle. Line prepared dish with this. Roll out remaining dough and set aside. Fill base with filling, then place pastry over the top. Pinch together with the bottom dough and roll this edge in on itself to seal. Brush with beaten egg, then make two or three small slashes on the surface with a sharp knife. Bake in oven until crust is golden, 50 to 60 minutes. Cool slightly before serving.

SERVES 4 TO 6

PAPPARDELLE WITH SUN-DRIED TOMATOES

½ red capsicum (pepper)

½ yellow capsicum (pepper)

3 tablespoons olive oil

3 spring onions, sliced

60 g (2 oz) ham, thinly sliced

1 small fresh red chilli, finely chopped

5 pieces sun-dried tomatoes in oil, drained and sliced

2 tablespoons extra virgin olive oil

freshly ground black pepper

600 g (1 lb 3 oz) fresh pappardelle or 400 g (13 oz) dried

1 tablespoon shredded fresh basil

1 Place capsicums under a hot grill and roast until skin is blackened and blistered.

When cooled, peel off skins, wipe clean and cut into strips.

2 Heat oil in a large frying pan and add onions, ham and chilli. Sauté briefly, then add dried tomatoes, oil and roasted peppers. Toss until heated through then season with pepper.

3 In the meantime, cook pappardelle in boiling salted water until *al dente*. Drain. Transfer to pan with sauce, add basil and toss lightly to combine. Divide between warmed pasta bowls and serve at once, accompanied by freshly grated Parmesan cheese.

SERVES 4

RISI E BISI

4 cups (1 litre/32 fl oz) vegetable or light chicken stock

2 tablespoons olive oil

1 small onion, finely chopped

2 tablespoons finely chopped parsley

1 ½ cups (300 g/10 oz) Arborio rice

300 g (10 oz) shelled young peas

salt and freshly ground pepper

30 g (1oz) butter

freshly grated Parmesan cheese

1 Put stock in a saucepan and bring to the boil. Keep hot, but not boiling.

2 Heat olive oil in a large saucepan and sauté onion until soft and golden. Stir in parsley, then rice. Cook, stirring, to coat rice well. Add a ladleful of stock and simmer until liquid is almost evaporated. Add another ladleful of stock, the peas, and salt and pepper to taste. Cook, stirring, until liquid has almost evaporated. Continue like this until the rice is tender but still *al dente*, and most of the liquid has evaporated. Add butter and stir until melted. Serve immediately, accompanied by the grated Parmesan.

SERVES 4

≈ **A MEAL OF RICE**

Perhaps the most important rice dish from the Veneto, Risi e Bisi (rice and peas in local dialect) always seems to be enjoyed by those not usually enamoured with rice. It is just the thing to knock up for a supper or luncheon where it only needs to be accompanied by crusty bread. It is best when made with small fresh young peas, and the consistency is rather like a thick soup, thick enough to be eaten with a fork.

STUFFED PASTA SHELLS WITH PRAWNS AND LEEKS

24 giant pasta shells

1 tablespoon butter

300 g (10 oz) trimmed leeks, thinly sliced

200 g (6½ oz) prawn (shrimp) or lobster meat

2 teaspoons fresh lemon juice

125 g (4 oz) ricotta cheese

salt and freshly ground black pepper

chives, to garnish

2 tablespoons grated Parmesan cheese

SAUCE
20 g (⅔ oz) butter

1 tablespoon plain (all-purpose) flour

1¾ cups (450 ml/15 fl oz) milk

2 tablespoons grated Parmesan cheese

salt and white pepper

1 Cook pasta shells in batches in boiling salted water until *al dente*. Drain well and set to one side. Discard any torn ones.

2 Heat butter in a frying pan and cook leeks, stirring, until soft. Add prawns and lemon juice and sauté for 2 to 3 minutes or until mixture is quite dry. Remove from heat and when cool, add ricotta. Toss to combine and season to taste with salt and pepper.

3 **TO PREPARE SAUCE:** Melt butter in a saucepan and stir in flour. Cook gently, stirring, for 15 to 20 seconds, then remove from heat. Stir in milk, return to heat and gently bring to the boil. When thickened, stir in Parmesan and season to taste with salt and pepper.

4 Pour a thin layer of sauce into a shallow heatproof dish. Stuff each shell with some of the prawn and leek mixture and arrange them in a single layer in the dish. Spoon over sauce, top with a few chopped chives and sprinkle Parmesan over the top. Place under a hot grill until golden brown. Serve at once.

SERVES 4 TO 6

BAKED STUFFED SARDINES

Fresh sardines and anchovies have that unmistakable essence of the Mediterranean, and they are prepared in so many different ways along the coastline of Italy that it's surely possible to have a plate of them every day for years, and each one would be unique! Here is a favourite which takes very little time to prepare.

½ cup (125 ml/4 fl oz) olive oil

12 fresh sardines

½ cup (60 g/2 oz) breadcrumbs

1 onion, finely chopped

1 clove garlic, finely minced

3 tablespoons pine nuts

1 tablespoon finely chopped fresh parsley

1 tablespoon finely chopped fresh chives

salt and freshly ground black pepper

juice 1 lemon

1 lemon, cut into wedges

1 Preheat oven to 200°C (400°F). Grease a shallow ovenproof dish with 1 tablespoon of the oil.

2 Cut heads off sardines and split each open down its belly. Turn skin side up on a board and press firmly down on its backbone. Lift out backbone and discard, then rinse body cavity and dry on paper towels.

3 Heat 4 tablespoons oil in a pan, add half the breadcrumbs and toss until golden. Add onion, lightly sauté 1 to 2 minutes, then add garlic and pine nuts. Sauté until pine nuts are golden. Remove from heat, stir in parsley and chives, and season with salt and pepper. Put some filling into the cavity of each sardine, then bring up sides and close off opened end with a skewer to form a boat shape.

4 Arrange sardines in a single layer in prepared dish, sprinkle reserved breadcrumbs on top and drizzle over the last of the oil. Bake until golden, about 20 minutes. Remove skewers. Squeeze lemon juice over the top and serve hot, accompanied by lemon wedges.

SERVES 4

ARTICHOKE, ZUCCHINI AND LEEK PIE

90 g (3 oz) butter

2 leeks, white part only, thinly sliced

2 zucchinis (courgettes), sliced

350 g (11 oz) canned drained artichoke hearts

salt and freshly ground black pepper

2 tablespoons grated Parmesan cheese

3 eggs, beaten

250 g (8 oz) puff pastry

1 tablespoon breadcrumbs

185 g (6 oz) Emmenthal or Jarlsberg cheese, thinly sliced

1 Preheat oven to 190°C (375°F) and grease a 22 cm (9 in) pie dish.

2 Heat half the butter and gently sauté leek rings until soft. Remove from pan and set aside. Add remaining butter and sauté zucchini until tender. Transfer zucchini to a blender or processor and add artichoke hearts. Blend to a thick pulp then season with salt and pepper. Transfer to a bowl and combine with Parmesan and eggs.

3 Roll out pastry and line prepared dish. Prick the base with a fork, sprinkle on breadcrumbs and layer sliced cheese over the top. Pour the artichoke mixture over cheese and arrange leek rings on the surface.

4 Bake for 30 to 40 minutes, or until pastry is cooked through and the filling set. Remove from oven and let rest for a few minutes before serving.

SERVES 6

STUFFED AND BAKED ARTICHOKES

2 young fresh artichokes with long stems

fresh lemon juice

salt

2 tablespoons breadcrumbs

2 tablespoons finely chopped fresh parsley

2 cloves garlic, minced

60 g (2 oz) lean bacon or ham

1 tomato, peeled, seeded and finely chopped

freshly ground black pepper

4 tablespoons olive oil

½ cup (125 ml/4 fl oz) dry white wine

1 Preheat oven to 160°C (325°F).

2 **TO PREPARE ARTICHOKES:** Snap off tough outside leaves and cut off one-quarter to one-third of the tops of those remaining. Peel the stem and remove the bottom ½ cm (¼ in) or so. Cut each one in half along its length to expose the choke and the white centre of the stem. Immediately squeeze lemon juice over all the cut surfaces. Scoop out the hairy choke and inedible mauve leaves with a spoon. Boil a large pan (not aluminium or iron) of water with a large pinch of salt and a good squeeze of lemon juice; plunge artichokes into it. Simmer for 20 minutes.

3 In the meantime, combine breadcrumbs, parsley, garlic, bacon and tomato, and salt and pepper to taste.

4 When the artichokes are just tender, remove from water and leave upside down on a teatowel to drain. Transfer to a rectangular ovenproof dish, cut side up, and fill the cavity with stuffing. Drizzle olive oil over the artichokes and add the wine to the dish. Cover, and bake in the oven for 30 minutes. Serve hot, with some of the pan juices drizzled over the top.

SERVES 4

≈ **ARTICHOKES IN ITALY**

Italians are very partial to artichokes and in spring, when the new season's crops hit the markets, they are feasted upon in restaurants and in the home with great entusiasmo. The large, globular Romanesco or Mammola type is most suitable for stuffing.

Tortellini with Pistachios and Basil

≈ COMBINING PASTA AND SAUCE

Most pasta dishes can be cooked using this method. If the sauce is to be fried or sautéed, do so in a wok or a frying pan large enough to take both sauce and the pasta once it's cooked. When the time comes to combine the two, drain the pasta and toss it through the sauce while it is still in the wok. Very quick, clean, and both pasta and sauce keep hot.

TORTELLINI WITH PISTACHIOS AND BASIL

600 g (1 lb 3 oz) cheese-filled tortellini
90 g (3 oz) butter
60 g (2 oz) shelled pistachio kernels, crushed
4 to 6 tablespoons cream
1 tablespoon finely chopped fresh basil
freshly ground Parmesan cheese
freshly ground black pepper

1 Put the tortellini on to cook in boiling salted water.

2 In the meantime, melt butter in a frying pan or wok and when it starts to go golden, stir in crushed pistachios. Cook over a low heat, stirring, 1 minute. Add 4 tablespoons cream and basil, and a few good grates of Parmesan. Taste for pepper. If the sauce becomes too thick, add more cream.

3 When tortellini is *al dente*, drain and add to frying pan. Toss to coat well, then transfer to warmed serving plates and serve at once. Pass around the Parmesan and pepper mill.

SERVES 4

ARTICHOKE GNOCCHI WITH CHEESE AND LEEK

GNOCCHI
250 g (8 oz) white bread, cubed
1 cup (250 ml/8 fl oz) dry white wine

3 ¼ cups (400 g/13 oz) plain (all-purpose) flour

pinch salt

6 tablespoons grated Parmesan cheese

4 artichoke hearts, finely minced

2 eggs, lightly beaten

SAUCE

3 tablespoons butter

1 leek, finely sliced

pinch nutmeg

salt and white pepper

¾ cup (180 ml/6 fl oz) cream

1 tablespoon grated Parmesan cheese

⅓ cup (40 g/1 ½ oz) grated mild cheese

2 to 3 sprigs fresh thyme

1 Preheat oven to 180°C (350°F). Grease a shallow ovenproof dish.

2 TO PREPARE GNOCCHI: Put bread in a bowl and pour in wine. Leave to soak for 10 minutes.

In a large bowl combine flour, salt and Parmesan. Add artichoke purée, eggs, and the bread/wine mixture. Knead well, adding more flour or a little water if neccessary to give a smooth, dry dough. Cover with plastic wrap and rest for 30 minutes.

3 TO PREPARE SAUCE: Melt butter in a saucepan and add leek, nutmeg, and season with salt and pepper. Gently sauté until leek is softened but not browned, then add cream. Bring to the boil and simmer until thickened, 8 to 10 minutes. Stir in cheeses and continue cooking until they melt. Keep warm.

4 Divide dough into 3 to 4 manageable pieces, then roll each into long cylinders about 1 cm (½ in) diameter. Cut these into 2 cm (1 in) lengths and press one side of each gnocchi over the tines of a fork to give a rigate (ridged) pattern.

5 Cook gnocchi in plenty of boiling, salted water until *al dente*. Drain and transfer to prepared dish. Pour the sauce over and arrange thyme on top. Bake for 20 minutes. Serve hot, accompanied by extra grated Parmesan cheese.

SERVES 4

Artichoke Gnocchi with Cheese and Leek

RED RADICCHIO PIE

This crustless pie is just the thing for a luncheon or light evening meal. Use the long, smooth leaved variety of radicchio known as red chicory or radicchio di Treviso, as it is more succulent and tender than the round globular type.

3 tablespoons breadcrumbs

3 tablespoons olive oil

60 g (2 oz) butter

1 large onion, finely sliced

1 clove garlic, minced

1 kg (2 lb) red radicchio with roots removed and leaves separated

salt and freshly ground black pepper

¾ cup (125 g/4 oz) rice

4 cups (1 litre/32 fl oz) light chicken stock

4 eggs

3 tablespoons freshly grated Parmesan cheese

1 tablespoon extra virgin olive oil

1 Preheat oven to 180°C (350°F). Grease a 24 cm (10 in) baking dish and sprinkle the surface with half the breadcrumbs.

2 Heat olive oil and butter in a large pan and add onion. Sauté gently until softened, then stir in garlic and radicchio. Lightly salt and pepper, cover, and cook over a low heat for 10 minutes.

3 Add rice and stir to coat for 1 to 2 minutes, then add stock. Bring to the boil and simmer, uncovered, until rice is *al dente* and most of the stock has evaporated, about 10 minutes. Remove from heat and cool.

4 Lightly beat eggs and Parmesan in a bowl then stir in radicchio mixture. Taste for salt and pepper. Transfer mixture to prepared dish and drizzle extra virgin olive oil over the surface. Sprinkle remaining breadcrumbs on top and bake in the oven until golden and set, about 45 minutes.

5 Let the pie cool before unmoulding. Serve warm.

SERVES 4 TO 6

LAMB PARCELS

Pasta parcels are economical and appetising, and they are a good way of using leftovers; one of the most tasty fillings is simply made from finely chopped leftover roast meat with its gravy.

4 tablespoons olive oil

1 onion, finely chopped

2 cloves garlic, minced

2 tablespoons pine nuts

600 g (1 lb 3 oz) lamb mince

¾ cup (200 ml/6 fl oz) dry red wine

200 g (6½ oz) drained canned tomatoes, seeded and chopped

1 tablespoon finely chopped fresh parsley

good pinch chilli flakes

2 cups (250 ml/8 fl oz) water

salt and freshly ground black pepper

2 tablespoons chopped fresh coriander

8 sheets lasagne pasta, fresh or dried, to measure approximately 16 cm (6 in) square when cooked

4 tablespoons cream

4 tablespoons grated Parmesan cheese

coriander sprigs, to garnish

1 Heat oil in a pan and sauté onion and garlic gently until onion softens. Add pine nuts and sauté until golden. Add lamb and cook, stirring often, until browned. Add wine and cook 5 minutes, then stir in tomatoes, parsley and chilli. Cook 1 to 2 minutes, add water, salt and pepper to taste, and coriander. Cook, partially covered, for 30 minutes or until sauce thickens.

2 In the meantime, carefully cook lasagne sheets, a few at a time, in plenty of boiling, salted water. Drain when *al dente* and lay out on a teatowel.

3 Spoon off about 4 tablespoons liquid from sauce and put in a small pan with cream (it doesn't matter if a few chunky bits of sauce get caught into it). Bring to the boil and simmer until slightly thickened. Keep warm.

4 When lamb is cooked, remove from heat. Divide between pasta sheets and fold each one up like an envelope to encase the filling. Place side by side with smooth surfaces up in a shallow heatproof dish. Spoon sauce over the top, and sprinkle on Parmesan.

5 Place under a hot grill until cheese melts and browns. Garnish with coriander sprigs and serve at once.

SERVES 4

PASTA SAUCE OF TUNA, ZUCCHINI AND SAFFRON

20 g (²⁄₃ oz) butter

1 onion, sliced

2 cloves garlic, minced

good pinch saffron powder

½ cup (125 ml/4 fl oz) chicken stock

½ cup (125 ml/4 fl oz) cream

salt and freshly ground black pepper

¼ teaspoon nutmeg

¼ teaspoon curry powder (optional)

3 zucchini (courgettes), cut into thin sticks 4 cm (2 in) long

400 g (13 oz) canned tuna, drained

1 Heat butter in a frying pan and cook onions and garlic over a low heat until soft. Add saffron and stir to coat. Add chicken stock and cream, bring to the boil and simmer until thickened. Add salt and pepper to taste and nutmeg, curry powder and zucchini. Simmer 1 minute, or until zucchini is cooked but still crisp. Toss through tuna, stirring to break up meat. When tuna is heated the sauce is ready.

This can be served on any flat or shaped pasta, although it is particularly good on trenette or linguine.

SERVES 4

CAPSICUM WITH SCRAMBLED EGGS

Serving scrambled eggs with vegetables is more common in those regions of Italy which have a history of Spanish occupation, and so the Spaniards are held responsible for this popular and tasty combination.

2 tomatoes

4 tablespoons olive oil

2 cloves garlic

1 large yellow capsicum (pepper), cut into short strips

1 large red capsicum (pepper), cut into short strips

5 to 6 small basil leaves

2 eggs

salt and freshly ground black pepper

½ tablespoon grated Parmesan cheese

1 Dip tomatoes into boiling water, then peel, seed and chop them.

2 Heat oil in a frying pan and gently sauté cloves garlic until brown. Discard. Add capsicums to pan and fry over a low heat until tender, about 10 minutes. Stir in tomatoes and basil and cook for a further 10 minutes.

3 Beat eggs with a good sprinkling of salt and pepper, then stir them into the pepper mixture. Keep stirring until eggs are lightly scrambled. Serve at once, sprinkled with the Parmesan.

SERVES 2 TO 4

≈ SCRAMBLED EGGS

Uniting a few ingredients by this scrambled egg method is a thrifty means of making a meal from those couple of vegetables remaining in the crisper.

MAIN MEALS

In Sardinia, for great occasions, a huge turkey might be stuffed with a duck, then a chicken, then a partridge, then a little lark or two ... and spit roasted. Although this may seem overabundant, it typifies the Italian attitude to birds and poultry of all kinds, they love them!

Mutton and lamb are also favourites. In Abruzzi the tender *castrato* (castrated mutton) is a speciality. In Rome it's spring lamb that's sought after, while in Lombardy lamb is often cooked together with veal, pork and chicken as in *bollito misti* and *fritti misti*, mixed boiled or mixed fried meats. Pork is popular with *porchetta* (roast suckling pig) said to have originated in the Marche, a beautiful region of mountains and rich pastures. Red meat is special in Tuscany, with the beef from the Chianina cattle of the Chiana Valley the most highly regarded. They are a huge, ancient breed which matures early and their flesh is tender and succulent.

In the south, seafood is often the main component of a meal as it is cheap and plentiful. Little sea-urchins, sea dates or newborn fish are enjoyed raw and it's common for seafood to be served cold.

Risotto with Zucchini and Scallops (page 46); Cold Baked Fish with Red Capsicum Mayonnaise (page 60); Chicken with Pancetta and Capsicum (page 60)

RISOTTO WITH ZUCCHINI AND SCALLOPS

9 cups (2¼ litres/72 fl oz) chicken stock (try to avoid using stock cubes as they become too salty)

60 g (2 oz) butter

3 tablespoons olive oil

1 onion, finely chopped

2 cups (450 g/14 oz) Arborio rice (see Glossary)

¾ cup (170 ml/6 fl oz) dry white wine

700 g (1 lb 6 oz) zucchini (courgettes), cut into 2 cm (¾ in) pieces

250 g (8 oz) sea scallops, coral left on and cut in half if large

⅔ cup (90 g/3 oz) grated Parmesan cheese

white pepper

1 Heat chicken stock in a saucepan and keep warm throughout.

2 In a large heavy-based saucepan heat butter and olive oil and gently sauté onion until soft, about 10 minutes. Add Arborio and cook, stirring, for 2 minutes or until the rice is well coated.

3 Add wine, bring to the boil and cook for 2 to 3 minutes or until the wine is absorbed. Add ¾ cup (170 ml/6 fl oz) warm stock and cook at a vigorous simmer, stirring, until it is absorbed. Continue to add stock, ¾ cup at a time, stirring and simmering for 3 to 5 minutes between each addition, and waiting for the stock to be absorbed before adding the next lot. When the rice begins to soften, you will have 4 to 6 cups (1 to 1½ litres/32 fl oz to 48 fl oz) of stock left. Add the zucchini and ½ cup (125 ml/4 fl oz) stock and proceed as before, but now adding ½ cup stock each time. When the rice is barely al dente there should be about 3 cups (750 ml/25 oz) left. Add the scallops, ½ cup stock and simmer and stir for 3 to 5 minutes. The mixture should now be creamy but the rice still *al dente*. If necessary, add more stock and continue in the same manner until the rice is ready.

4 Remove the pan from the heat, stir in the Parmesan cheese and pepper to taste, and transfer to a warm serving dish. Serve immediately.

SERVES 6

POT-ROASTED VEAL WITH TWO MUSHROOMS

10 g (½ oz) dried porcini mushrooms

40 g (1½ oz) butter

2 tablespoons extra virgin olive oil

2 kg (4 lb) veal roast

2 cloves garlic

2 large sprigs fresh rosemary

salt and freshly ground black pepper

200 g (6½ oz) fresh large button mushrooms, sliced

1 cup (250 ml/8 fl oz) white wine

1 Soak dried porcini in 1 cup (250 ml/ 8 fl oz) of warm water for 30 minutes.

2 In a large heatproof casserole or Dutch oven heat the butter and oil. Add the veal, garlic and rosemary, season well with salt and pepper, then brown meat on all sides over a medium heat.

3 Add fresh mushrooms, wine, and half the water that the porcini have been soaking in. Bring to the boil and simmer 5 minutes.

4 Add porcini, reserving the remaining liquid. Cover the pot, leaving a slight gap for evaporation. Lower heat and simmer, turning 2 or 3 times, for 1 hour or until juices run clear from the meat when pricked. If it appears to be losing too much liquid as it cooks, add extra wine and cover over pot a little more.

5 Remove veal, transfer to a warm plate and discard cloves garlic and rosemary. Increase heat under pot, add reserved porcini liquid and boil rapidly until sauce thickens.

6 Slice meat, pour over sauce and serve immediately.

SERVES 6 TO 8

LAMB WITH FRESH ARTICHOKES

1 boned leg of lamb, cut into 4 cm (1½ in) cubes

plain (all-purpose) flour, seasoned

4 tablespoons olive oil

90 g (3 oz) butter

2 cloves garlic

½ teaspoon dried sage

½ cup (125 ml/4 fl oz) Marsala

300 g (10 oz) tomatoes, peeled, seeded and chopped

⅔ cup (150 ml/5 fl oz) light beef stock

small piece lemon rind

salt and freshly ground black pepper

4 small fresh artichokes

juice ½ lemon

1 clove garlic, minced

⅔ cup (150 ml/5 fl oz) boiling water

12 pitted black olives

fresh sage leaves for garnish (optional)

1 Toss lamb in seasoned flour to coat.

2 Heat half the oil and half the butter in a heatproof casserole and add garlic cloves. Sauté for 1 to 2 minutes, then add dried sage and lamb. Discard garlic. Cook, stirring from time to time, until lamb is browned. Pour on Marsala and cook until it has nearly all evaporated, then stir in tomatoes and stock. Add lemon rind and season with salt and pepper. Cover pan and cook over a moderate heat for 1 hour, adding a little more stock if necessary.

3 In the meantime, remove the ends of the stalks and outer leaves from artichokes. Trim off one-quarter to one-third of the tips of the leaves, and then force them open to remove the chokes with a spoon. Place in a bowl of water with lemon juice as each one is cut. Heat remaining oil and butter in a frying pan (not aluminium) and add garlic. Cut each artichoke into 6 pieces along its length and add to garlic in pan. Sauté briefly, then pour in boiling water. Season with salt and pepper. Cover and cook over a moderate heat until just tender. Transfer to lamb pot, stir through and cook for a further 15 to 20 minutes.

4 When ready to serve, check seasoning, then arrange meat in a warm dish with the sauce and olives. Garnish with fresh sage, and serve with boiled rice or mashed potatoes.

SERVES 6

CHICKEN BREASTS WITH BOCCONCINI AND OLIVES

4 small chicken breasts, boned and skinned

plain (all-purpose) flour, seasoned

40 g (1½ oz) butter

2 tablespoons olive oil

1 tablespoon brandy

90 g (3 oz) bocconcini or other fresh mozzarella, thinly sliced

4 tablespoons black or green olive paste

1 Trim chicken and fold out fillet to give an evenly flat breast. Toss in seasoned flour to lightly coat.

2 Melt butter and olive oil in a heavy-based frying pan and gently brown chicken. Add brandy to pan juices, cook until bubbling, then cover pan and poach chicken until tender.

3 Top each breast with a layer of cheese, and spread olive paste on top. Reduce heat to very low, re-cover pan and wait for the cheese to melt. Serve at once, accompanied by boiled baby potatoes.

SERVES 4

*Chicken with Mushrooms
and Sun-dried Tomatoes;
Pork with Fennel
and Leeks*

PORK WITH FENNEL AND LEEKS

*Using the minimum of seasoning, this succulent pot-roast
relies on the inherent flavour of the ingredients and slow,
even cooking. It is perfectly complimented by green peas.*

**1 to 1½ kg (2 to 3 lb) pork loin roast, either
rolled or with tail removed**

salt and finely ground black pepper

3 tablespoons vegetable oil

2 tablespoons olive oil

2 leeks, trimmed and sliced

**1 fennel bulb, trimmed and sliced (reserve
some green sprigs off the top for garnish)**

1 cup (250 ml/8 fl oz) water

2 tablespoons cream

1 Season pork with salt and pepper.

2 Heat vegetable and olive oil in a deep
heatproof casserole and evenly brown pork
on all sides. Remove from pan.

3 Add leek and fennel slices to oil and cook,
stirring often, until softened and golden,
8 to 10 minutes.

4 Return pork to pan, add water and bring
to the boil. Reduce heat and simmer,
covered, until juices run clear when
skewered, about 1 hour.

5 Transfer pork to a warm platter. Increase
heat in pan and quickly thicken sauce, if
necessary. Stir in cream.

6 Slice pork and serve on a bed of leeks and
fennel, garnished with reserved fennel sprigs.
Green peas make a good side dish.

SERVES 4

POLLO ALLA TORINESE

Turin, the capital of Piemonte, is the home of vermouth. Made from white wine blended with spirits, herbs and bitters, this apperitif has been manufactured there commercially since the eighteenth century. Dry white vermouth is used instead of white wine in recipes and is particularly good with chicken, veal and fish.

1 lemon

1½ kg (3 lb) chicken

2 cloves garlic, sliced in half

salt and freshly ground black pepper

60 g (2 oz) butter

1¼ cups (325 ml/11 fl oz) Cinzano Bianco or other white vermouth

1 cup (250 ml/8 fl oz) cream

2 tablespoons finely chopped fresh parsley and coriander

1 Preheat oven to 180°C (350°F).

2 Peel one-third of the lemon, reserving strips of peel, then squeeze juice to get 4 tablespoons.

3 Truss chicken and place lemon peel and garlic in the cavity. Season well with salt and pepper.

4 On the stove top, melt butter in a heavy baking dish and brown chicken on all sides. Remove chicken and pour in ¾ cup (200 ml/6½ fl oz) of Cinzano. Boil to reduce by a quarter. Return chicken, pour over juices, then bake, uncovered, for 1 hour or until juices run clear when pricked. From time to time baste with pan juices.

5 Remove dish from oven and cut chicken into portions. Place on a serving platter and keep warm. Return dish to stove top, add remaining Cinzano and reduce by half over a strong heat. Stir in lemon juice and cream, and bubble fiercely to thicken. Taste for seasoning, then spoon over chicken and sprinkle on the parsley and coriander. Serve immediately, accompanied by steamed rice or roasted potatoes.

SERVES 4

CHICKEN WITH MUSHROOMS AND SUN-DRIED TOMATOES

3 tablespoons olive oil

60 g (2 oz) butter

2 kg (4 lb) chicken, cut into serving size pieces

1 onion, finely chopped

2 whole cloves garlic

250 g (8 oz) button mushrooms, thickly sliced

1 tablespoon mixed finely chopped fresh herbs, e.g. basil, sage, oregano, parsley

salt and freshly ground black pepper

½ cup (125 ml/4 fl oz) white wine

¾ cup (200 ml/6½ fl oz) chicken stock

2 tablespoons plain (all-purpose) flour

¾ cup (200 ml/6½ fl oz) cream

⅓ cup (100 g/3½ oz) sun-dried tomatoes which have been marinated in olive oil

1 Heat oil and butter in a deep heatproof casserole. Sauté chicken pieces until brown on all sides. Remove from pan and set to one side.

2 Add onion and garlic to pan and sauté until golden, about 10 minutes, stirring often.

3 Add mushrooms and herbs, toss to coat and season with salt and pepper. Discard cloves garlic.

4 Pour in wine and reduce quickly over a high heat. Stir in stock, bring to the boil then reduce heat.

5 Blend flour with cream and gradually stir into pan. Cook gently, stirring often until sauce has thickened.

6 Return chicken to pan and stir in dried tomatoes. Cook over moderate heat for 10 to 15 minutes.

SERVES 4

≈ TIME-SAVER

In Chicken with Mushrooms and Sun-dried Tomatoes, a barbecued chicken can be substituted for the fresh one when time is pressing. Just reduce by half the amount of oil and butter to sauté the onion and garlic, and stir in the chicken pieces after the cream has been added and the sauce thickens. If using dried tomatoes, i.e those which haven't been marinated and have not been reconstituted, add them to the pan along with the mushrooms and herbs.

FILLET STEAK WITH ORANGE AND BALSAMIC VINEGAR

No time to cook but need an impressive dish? Here's a sure-fire solution taking 10 minutes at the most and using only 6 ingredients, including pepper and salt! The quality of balsamic vinegar really makes a difference and like wine, price is a fair indication of worth. The cheaper balsamic vinegars bear a fleeting resemblance to those which bear the Seal of Guarantee of the Consorzio Tra Produttori Dell'Aceto Balsamico Traditionale di Modena — quite a mouthful — the best of which can fetch hundreds of thousands of lire for just 100 ml (3 fl oz).

salt and freshly ground black pepper
4 beef fillet steaks
40 g (1 ½ oz) butter
1 orange
balsamic vinegar

1 Lightly salt and pepper both sides of each fillet.

2 Melt butter in a frying pan (preferably a griddled one) and when bubbling, add fillets. Fry quickly on each side to seal and brown, then remove pan from heat and rest 2 to 3 minutes. Some juice will be released into the pan as the meat cools slightly.

3 Meanwhile, take a small sharp knife and thinly peel two-thirds of the orange. Remove all pith from this, and slice thinly into julienne. Add to pan, then replace it over heat. Squeeze in 1 to 2 teaspoons orange juice, followed by about 1 teaspoon of balsamic vinegar. Depending on how well cooked the steaks are to be, proceed as desired. Turn the fillets over once and in doing so give them a half turn; this will create a cross grid effect if using a griddled pan. Add one or two drops more orange juice, and balsamic vinegar to keep the pan juices flowing. When cooked to desired degree, taste sauce for balance of flavours, bearing in mind that quite a strong orange taste will come from the orange peel when bitten into. Serve immediately onto warmed plates, and spoon the pan juices and peel on top.

SERVES 4

VEAL WITH PROSCIUTTO AND VERMOUTH

8 slices veal scallopine
salt and freshly ground black pepper
8 thin slices prosciutto
8 fresh sage leaves
60 g (2 oz) butter
1 tablespoon olive oil
¾ cup (175 ml/6 fl oz) red vermouth
4 tablespoons cream

1 If the butcher hasn't already done so, pound the veal lightly between 2 pieces of plastic wrap. Trim edges to a neat shape. Season with a little salt and a few good grinds of pepper. Trim prosciutto slices to match veal, then secure one slice on the top of each scallopine along with one sage leaf, using wooden toothpicks.

2 Melt butter and oil in a large frying pan, then begin to fry scallopine with the prosciutto side down first, a few at a time. When veal is cooked and golden on both sides, transfer to a warm serving platter. Remove toothpicks.

3 Add vermouth to the pan juices and scrape up residue from the pan bottom. Simmer until sauce reduces by a third, then stir in cream. Continue simmering until sauce is thickened, then pour over veal and serve at once.

SERVES 4

Fillet Steak with Orange and Balsamic Vinegar (bottom); Veal with Prosciutto and Vermouth (top)

ALESSI TRAY FROM VENTURA IMPORTS, TABLE FROM ART OF STONE

GRILLED LOBSTER TAILS
WITH BASIL BUTTER

150 g (5 oz) butter, softened

3 tablespoons finely chopped fresh basil

**1 tablespoon finely chopped pistachio
kernels**

1 teaspoon grated orange zest

**4 small lobster tails, or other shellfish
in the shell**

2 tablespoons fresh lemon juice

2 tablespoons extra virgin olive oil

2 tablespoons shredded fresh basil

salt and ground white pepper

1 Combine butter, chopped basil, pistachios
and orange zest in a bowl and beat to
combine. Transfer to a small bowl and
refrigerate.

2 Split lobster shells down the underside,
fold back to the main shell at the sides and
remove, exposing the flesh.

3 Combine lemon juice, oil and shredded
basil, and salt and pepper. Brush each lobster

OSSOBUCO PIEMONTESE

125 g (4 oz) butter

½ cup (125 ml/4 fl oz) olive oil

2 onions, sliced then roughly chopped

2 medium red capsicums (peppers), cleaned and cut into chunks

12 ossobuco pieces

plain (all-purpose) flour, seasoned

1 cup (250 ml/8 fl oz) dry white wine

1 kg (2 lb) tomatoes (either fresh or canned), peeled, seeded and chopped

½ teaspoon salt

1 teaspoon freshly ground black pepper

1 teaspoon finely chopped garlic

1 teaspoon dried basil

1 teaspoon dried oregano

1 tablespoon tomato paste

1 Melt half the butter and olive oil in a large heatproof pot or Dutch oven. Sauté onions gently until golden, about 10 minutes. Add capsicums and sauté over a low heat for a further 5 minutes. Remove from pot and set aside.

2 Toss ossobuco in seasoned flour.

3 Put remaining butter and oil in the pot and when bubbling, add ossobuco, a few at a time. Cook gently until brown on all sides. Pour in wine and cook over a high heat for 5 to 6 minutes, stirring frequently to deglaze the pot. Add tomatoes, salt, pepper, garlic, basil and oregano and return onion and pepper mixture to pot. Stir in tomato paste. Cover and cook over a low heat for 1½ hours, or until meat is tender but still remaining on the bone.

4 Adjust seasoning if necessary before serving. Serve with creamy baked polenta or mashed potatoes.

SERVES 4 TO 6

≈ **OSSOBUCO**

Ossobuco (or Ossibuchi) are veal shanks which have been cut across into pieces at least 4 cm (1½ in) thick. The meat should be pale pink in colour, but with the shanks of a good size to yield the maximum marrow. This marrow is an added bonus and there are special marrow spoons (nicknamed tax agents, as they take everything right down to the bone!) for fishing it out. If you don't happen to have a supply of these at home, short-handled fondue forks or parfait spoons work very well.

tail generously with mixture, place on a plate and refrigerate, covered, for 1 hour.

4 Put tails flesh side up about 10 cm (4 in) below a moderate grill. Cook until lightly browned, turn, and grill with shell uppermost for 3 to 4 minutes. Turn once more and cook until flesh is cooked through. Transfer at once to warmed plates, place a spoonful of basil butter on top of each one and serve as the butter begins to melt. Hand around the butter bowl for extra lashings.

SERVES 4

FETTUCCINE ALLA FIORENTINA

Recipes which include spinach have come to be called alla Fiorentina because of the Florentine's partiality to spinach. In this dish the perch used can either be freshwater or from the sea.

BECHAMEL SAUCE

100 g (3½ oz) butter

5 tablespoons plain (all-purpose) flour

1 teaspoon salt

large pinch white pepper

pinch nutmeg

2½ cups (625 ml/20 fl oz) milk

1 bay leaf

12 small perch fillets

1 teaspoon salt

¼ teaspoon white pepper

2 cups (500 ml/16 fl oz) dry white wine

1 kg (2 lb) fresh spinach leaves (need about 600 g/1 lb 3 oz when cooked)

500 g (1 lb) fresh fettuccine, or 350 g (11 oz) dried, cooked

1 tablespoon olive oil

2 tablespoons grated Parmesan cheese

1 Preheat oven to 200°C (400°F).

2 TO PREPARE BECHAMEL SAUCE: Melt butter in a saucepan. Blend in flour, stir for 10 to 12 seconds, then stir in salt, pepper and nutmeg. Gradually add milk, stirring until smooth. Add bay leaf and bring to the boil. Simmer, stirring often, until thickened. Remove from heat.

3 Place perch fillets in a large pan, sprinkle with salt and pepper and pour over the wine. Bring to the boil and simmer until fish is just opaque. Gently remove from pan, keeping the fillets intact.

4 Rinse spinach and place in large pan with no more water than remains on the leaves. Cover and cook quickly until tender, about 5 minutes. Drain well and chop.

5 Grease a large baking dish or casserole with oil. Arrange half the spinach across the bottom, cover with half the cooked fettuccine and top with 6 perch fillets. Repeat layering. Pour bechamel sauce over the top then sprinkle with Parmesan cheese. Bake for 25 to 30 minutes.

SERVES 6

BAKED TUNA WITH OLIVES AND HERBS

3 tablespoons extra virgin olive oil

2 onions, sliced thinly

2 cloves garlic, finely chopped

200 g (6½ oz) Ligurian, Riviera or Niçoise olives, pitted

1 tablespoon white wine vinegar

1 tablespoon fresh chopped, or 1 teaspoon dried marjoram

salt and freshly ground black pepper

1 teaspoon olive oil, extra

4 tuna steaks, about 3 cm (1½ in) thick

1 tablespoon chopped fresh basil and parsley combined

1 Preheat oven to 180°C (350°F).

2 Heat 3 tablespoons oil in a large frying pan. Add onions and garlic and cook gently for 10 minutes, stirring often. Add olives, vinegar, marjoram and salt and pepper to taste and cook a further 2 to 3 minutes.

3 Grease a baking dish with 1 teaspoon of oil, and arrange tuna in a single layer across the bottom. Lightly salt and pepper them before spooning over the onion and olive sauce. Cover with foil and bake 15 minutes, or until tuna is just cooked through but still moist. Transfer to a warm serving plate, spoon the sauce over and sprinkle with basil and parsley.

SERVES 4

Baked Tuna with Olives and Herbs

*A salad of vegetables and
seafood piled high on a
platter with a garlic and
anchovy sauce; this
visually extravagant
Genoese dish may take a
little time to compile, but
once prepared there is
nothing left to do but slice
some crusty bread. It is
just the thing to feed a
crowd for lunch on a
summer's day, or to be the
starring attraction of a
special buffet. To get the
selection of vegetables and
seafood needed, it is only
worth doing for more
than 8 people.*

*Any small game will be
successful in this recipe
and it adapts well to
lamb. If black olive paste
is unavailable, stone
12 black olives and
roughly chop the flesh.*

CAPPON MAGRO

½ cup (125 ml/4 fl oz) olive oil

2 cloves garlic

12 thick slices white bread, crusts removed

a little white wine vinegar

200 g (6½ oz) each of a selection of 6 to 8 vegetables in season giving a variety of colour and texture e.g. carrots, potatoes, broccoli, zucchini (courgettes), green beans, artichokes

1 head celery, diced

1¾ cups (400 ml/13 oz) vinaigrette dressing

2 kg (4 lb) of a selection of seafood including prawns (shrimps), oysters, mussels, lobster, scallops and some-firm fleshed white fish

SAUCE

3 tablespoons pine nuts

3 cloves garlic

4 anchovy fillets

1 large bunch parsley, finely chopped

1 tablespoon capers

6 green olives, pitted

yolks of 2 hard-boiled eggs

2 tablespoons white wine vinegar

1 cup (250 ml/8 fl oz) olive oil

GARNISH

4 hard-boiled eggs, sliced lengthways

black olives, preferably small Ligurian or Niçoise

1 Preheat oven to 150 °C (300°F).

2 Heat olive oil in a small saucepan with garlic. Lightly brush bread slices on both sides with this before placing in oven to crisp. Paint with a little vinegar, set aside.

3 Prepare vegetables and cut into largish bite-size pieces. Boil or steam those which need to be cooked until *al dente*. Place in a large bowl with celery and half the vinaigrette and toss lightly.

4 Poach seafood which needs to be cooked, until just done. Remove shells from shellfish and cut fish into big bite-sized pieces. Place all in a bowl and toss lightly with remaining vinaigrette.

5 **TO PREPARE SAUCE:** Put all ingredients except vinegar and oil into a blender or processor and blend until smooth. Add vinegar, and then gradually pour in oil until a thick creamy consistency is reached.

6 **TO ASSEMBLE:** Arrange bread slices over a large serving platter and pour a little sauce on top. Then arrange the vegetables in a pile in the middle, surrounded by the assorted seafood. Go for height and colour combinations in arranging. Pour remaining sauce over the top and garnish with egg slices and olives.

SERVES 8 TO 10

RABBIT WITH OREGANO AND BLACK OLIVE PASTE

4 tablespoons olive oil

3 cloves garlic, minced

1½ kg (3 lb) rabbit pieces

1 tablespoon finely chopped fresh oregano, or ½ tablespoon dried

½ tablespoon finely chopped fresh mint

400 g (13 oz) canned peeled tomatoes, drained, squeezed free of seeds and chopped

2 to 3 tablespoons black olive paste or pâté

¾ cup (180 ml/6 fl oz) dry white wine

salt and freshly ground black pepper

1 Heat oil in a casserole or Dutch oven and add garlic. Toss for a few seconds, then add rabbit pieces. Cook, stirring often, until browned on all sides. Stir in oregano, mint, tomatoes, 2 tablespoons olive paste and wine. Cook for 2 to 3 minutes over a high heat, then cover and cook gently until meat is tender and sauce thickened, about 45 minutes. Add more olive paste if desired, and if necessary, lightly salt and pepper before serving.

SERVES 4

LAMB CUTLETS IN AN OLIVE AND PARMESAN CRUST

1 egg

2 tablespoons green olive paste

¼ cup (30 g/1 oz) breadcrumbs

5 tablespoons grated Parmesan cheese

8 lamb cutlets, trimmed of all fat

4 to 5 tabespoons plain (all-purpose) flour, seasoned with salt and pepper

60 g (2 oz) butter

3 tablespoons vegetable oil

1 Beat egg and stir in olive paste.

2 Combine breadcrumbs and Parmesan.

3 Coat each cutlet in seasoned flour, dip in egg mixture, then coat with Parmesan/ breadcrumbs. This can be done up to 4 hours ahead and kept refrigerated.

4 Heat butter and oil in a frying pan and cook cutlets over a medium heat until the crust is golden on both sides, 4 to 5 minutes. Briefly drain on a paper towel before serving.

SERVES 4

Lamb Cutlets in an Olive and Parmesan Crust

SCOTTIGLIA

¾ cup (180ml/6 fl oz) olive oil

3 onions, roughly chopped

2 carrots, chopped

2 stalks celery, chopped

4 cloves garlic, minced

3 tablespoons chopped fresh parsley

5 kg (10 lb) mixed poultry, game and meats, at least 8 different sorts e.g. quail, spatchcock, guinea fowl, lamb, beef, pork, rabbit etc

½ cup (125 ml/4 fl oz) fresh lemon juice

1¼ cups (300 ml/10 fl oz) dry red wine

800 g (1 lb 9 oz) peeled tomatoes, seeded and finely chopped

½ teaspoon mixed spice

2 fresh bay leaves or 2 lemon leaves

salt and freshly ground black pepper

chilli flakes, to taste

¾ cup (180 ml/6 fl oz) chicken or light beef stock

8 to 10 pieces garlic toast (see Bruschetta, page 10)

4 tablespoons finely chopped fresh parsley

lemon wedges

1 Heat half the olive oil in a large heatproof casserole or Dutch oven. Add onions, carrots, celery, garlic and parsley and sauté over a moderate heat for 5 minutes.

2 In the meantime, prepare meats by cutting those which have bones into chunks or cutlets, and the boneless into cubes of about 4 cm (1½ in).

3 When vegetables are softened, add the meats in batches and brown on all sides. Return all the pieces to the pot and add lemon juice. Bring to the boil and simmer for 1 to 2 minutes, then stir in wine. Bring back to the boil and simmer for 10 minutes.

4 Add tomatoes, mixed spice and bay leaves. Cover and cook over a low heat for 30 minutes. Season with salt and pepper and add chilli and stock. Return to the boil, cover, and cook a further 15 minutes. If the sauce is a little thin at this stage, increase heat, remove lid and reduce until thickened. (There won't be a lot of sauce, and it shouldn't be runny.)

5 Arrange garlic toast over a large deep-sided serving platter. Pile the contents of casserole over the centre, sprinkle the top with chopped parsley and serve with lemon wedges.

SERVES 8 TO 10

QUAIL WITH GARLIC, SAGE AND BRANDY

6 prepared quail

salt and freshly ground black pepper

2 tablespoons olive oil

40 g (1½ oz) butter

3 cloves garlic, peeled

1 tablespoon lightly packed fresh sage leaves, or ¼ teaspoon dried

½ cup (125 ml/4 fl oz) brandy

1 Split each bird from top to tail down its breast and open out flat. Season skins with salt and pepper.

2 Heat oil and butter in a large frying pan and sauté garlic for 2 to 3 minutes. When golden, discard. Add sage and quail, skin side down, and cook over a moderate heat until browned. Turn over and cook until done, moving them around in the pan from time to time.

3 Warm brandy in a small saucepan. Pour over quail and carefully ignite with a taper or match. Shake pan to keep quail moving until the flames go out. Serve immediately on a bed of grilled polenta or garlic toasts, and don't forget finger bowls!

SERVES 4

AGNELLO PASQUALINO

This lamb dish from Apulia combines two classically Easter ingredients, lamb and eggs, but in an unconventional way.

3 tablespoons olive oil

40 g (1 ½ oz) butter

2 onions, sliced

1 kg (2 lb) boned lean lamb, cubed

1 large sprig fresh mint

salt and freshly ground black pepper

¾ cup (180 ml/6 fl oz) dry white wine

500 g (1 lb) shelled fresh peas

3 eggs, beaten

4 tablespoons grated Parmesan cheese

3 tablespoons finely chopped fresh parsley

1 Heat oil and butter in a Dutch oven or deep heatproof casserole, add onions and cook gently until golden.

2 Add lamb and mint sprig, season with salt and pepper and cook until lamb is browned. Increase heat, add wine and cook until the alcohol has evaporated. Cover tightly, lower heat and simmer for 20 minutes. Add peas and cook, covered, for a further 20 minutes.

3 Combine eggs, Parmesan and parsley in a bowl and whisk to combine.

4 When ready to serve, remove pot from heat, discard mint sprig and pour the egg mixture over the meat. Put the lid back on. As soon as the eggs have set, serve.

SERVES 4 TO 6

Quail with Garlic, Sage and Brandy

BAKED FISH SERVED COLD WITH RED CAPSICUM MAYONNAISE

Although a fair amount of time is required to complete this dish, the actual preparation is easy and doesn't take too long; in fact it can be prepared the day before, chilled overnight then served at room temperature for a lunch or evening meal on a hot summer's day. The mayonnaise will be richer and sweeter if the caspicum is first roasted and peeled.

1 clove garlic, minced

2 tablespoons finely chopped fresh parsley

2 tablespoons finely chopped fresh basil

1 sprig rosemary, finely chopped

salt and freshly ground black pepper

2 tablespoons fresh lemon juice

5 tablespoons olive oil

1 whole white-fleshed fish suitable for baking, gutted and scaled

2 onions, finely sliced

4 tablespoons dry white wine

pea greens or watercress, to garnish

RED CAPSICUM MAYONNAISE

1 large red capsicum (pepper)

1 clove garlic

1 egg yolk

⅔ cup (150 ml/5 fl oz) extra virgin olive oil

salt and white pepper

1 Preheat oven to 180°C (350°F).

2 Combine garlic, parsley, basil and rosemary and season with salt and pepper. Moisten with lemon juice and 1 tablespoon of olive oil. Spread mixture throughout the cavity of the fish.

3 Lay onion slices out along the centre of a large rectangle of heavy-duty foil. Pour the remaining oil over them, then place fish on top. Season surface with salt and pepper and pour over wine. Fold up sides of foil and seal tightly, checking that there are no holes. Place parcel in a baking dish and transfer to

the oven. Bake for 30 minutes. Remove and allow to cool without unsealing the foil.

4 TO PREPARE MAYONNAISE: Purée capsicum in a blender or processor. Remove and squeeze dry in a teatowel. Put garlic and egg yolk in processor and blend, gradually adding olive oil. Add two-thirds of capsicum purée, taste for salt and pepper and add more purée if liked.

5 About 30 minutes before serving, remove fish from foil and arrange on a serving platter with the onion slices, greens and lemon wedges. Gently remove the skin from the uppermost side and discard.

6 Strain the juices left in the foil and boil down to thicken. Set aside to cool slightly then stir to taste into mayonnaise. Serve as an accompaniment to the fish.

SERVES 4 TO 6

CHICKEN WITH PANCETTA AND CAPSICUM

By smothering chicken with pancetta and capsicum their moisture and flavour is absorbed to give a subtle and succulent dish. Preferably use free-range chickens if available. The Italians call these pollo ruspante, *beautifully described as 'the chicken that scratches the ground to find its food'.*

2 tablespoons olive oil

40 g (1½ oz) butter

2 kg (4 lb) fresh chicken, cut into 4 to 6 pieces

2 red capsicum (peppers), thinly sliced

2 yellow capsicum (peppers), thinly sliced

2 cloves garlic, whole

2 small red chillis

225 g (7 oz) rolled pancetta or lean bacon

1 Heat oil and butter in a large, heavy-based casserole or Dutch oven. Lightly brown chicken pieces on all sides, then remove from pot. Add capsicum and sauté until soft, 6 to 8 minutes.

Chicken with Pancetta and Capsicum

2 Return chicken to pot, burying the pieces under capsicum. Add garlic and chillis. Layer the pancetta over capsicum to completely cover, then cover pot. Reduce heat to very low and braise for 30 minutes, or until meat is tender. Discard chillis and garlic cloves.

3 To serve, arrange chicken pieces on warmed plates, spoon over some capsicum and give each portion one or two slices of pancetta. Serve with polenta or rice.

SERVES 4

≈ SUBSTITUTE FOR CHICKEN

This method of cooking works equally well with turkey and most other poultry, but not duck, which is invariably too fatty.

VEGETABLES

Inhabitants of Tuscany are known by other Italians as *Mangiafagioli* (the Bean Eaters), and their beloved white bean turns up in all courses. In Rome too, beans of all types are as popular as the artichoke, and salad greens are so plentiful that a bowl of mixed salad is referred to as *tutto giardino* ... with the whole garden! In Venice, vegetables arrive from the mainland by the colourful boatload, while in the fertile plain around Novara in Piedmonte artichokes and capsicum (peppers) flourish, huge crops of asparagus appear in spring and in the hills the prized white truffles are gathered in autumn.

In Umbria, truffles are so plentiful they're treated with much less reverence than elsewhere and are used fresh, frozen, preserved or even ground to a paste, while mushrooms, chestnuts and wild celery are also favourites. In the south vegetables are a dominant part of the cooking style.

Pasta is often served with a vegetable sauce ... eggplants (aubergines), capsicum (peppers) and in particular tomatoes typify the cuisine. Throughout the country vegetables are served as a separate course and quite often make up a complete light meal. Cold, they grace a variety of salads, and of course they are an integral part of the celebrated antipasti course.

Front to back: Fried Plum Tomatoes (page 66); Summer Salad with Roasted Garlic Dressing (page 76); Tuscan Baked Potatoes (page 66)

GLASSES FROM ORREFORS KOSTA BODA. BOWL FROM CYDONIA THE GLASS STUDIO, PLATE FROM PILLIVUYT

POTATO PANCAKE

500 g (1 lb) potatoes, peeled

2 tablespoons grated Parmesan cheese

2 tablespoons plain (all-purpose) flour

1 tablespoon finely chopped fresh parsley

1 egg

salt and freshly ground black pepper

3 tablespoons olive oil

1 Roughly grate potatoes and place in a bowl with Parmesan, flour, parsley and egg. Mix well and season to taste with salt and pepper.

2 Heat oil in a large heavy-based frying pan. Add potato mixture and flatten it out evenly. Fry over a moderate heat until the bottom is set and golden. From time to time move it around in the pan to prevent it sticking.

3 In the meantime, turn on griller to high. Place pancake on a shelf 30 cm (12 in) below heat and grill until the top is golden, about 6 minutes. Cut into wedges and serve at once.

SERVES 2 TO 4

SPINACH WITH RAISINS AND PINE NUTS

Of Roman origin, this classic vegetable dish is still a great accompaniment to meat courses, but it is so easy and versatile that it has become a favourite antipasti dish as well. Leftovers can be quickly turned into a frittata by stirring through some eggs, and this is also delicious served cold.

1 kg (2 lb) English spinach or silverbeet leaves, no stems

pinch salt

2 tablespoons olive oil

20 g (⅔ oz) butter

3 tablespoons raisins

4 tablespoons pine nuts

1 to 2 tablespoons extra virgin olive oil

1 Rinse spinach thoroughly to remove dirt and grit, then shake off water. Place in a saucepan with only the water that remains on the leaves and salt, and cook over a low heat until wilted. Drain and let cool slightly before squeezing dry in a teatowel. Set aside.

2 Heat olive oil and butter in a frying pan and sauté raisins and pine nuts gently until pine nuts are golden. Add spinach and enough oil to coat it well. Sauté until spinach is heated and the flavours combined.

SERVES 4

ARTICHOKE HEARTS WITH TOMATO AND PARMESAN

This dish takes minutes to prepare, looks classy and can be served as an accompanying vegetable, or alone as a light meal.

olive oil

800 g (1½ lb) canned artichoke hearts, drained

3 large tomatoes, sliced

salt and freshly ground black pepper

½ cup (60 g/2 oz) grated Cheddar cheese

½ cup (60 g/2 oz) grated Parmesan cheese

1 Preheat oven to 180°C (350°F).

2 Cut artichokes into 3 to 4 slices lengthways. Lightly coat a shallow 25 cm x 15 cm (10 in x 6 in) ovenproof dish with olive oil.

3 Starting at one end of the dish, arrange alternating lines of artichoke heart and tomato slices.

4 Drizzle over some more olive oil, season with salt and pepper and cover first with the grated Cheddar and then the Parmesan.

5 Place in the oven and bake, uncovered, until the cheese is melted and browned, about 2 to 5 minutes.

SERVES 2 TO 4

Potato Pancake; Spinach with Raisins & Pine Nuts

TUSCAN BAKED POTATOES

This recipe is just what Tuscan food is all about; a few good quality ingredients, simply prepared and with an understated elegance. It can be made more rustic by increasing the size the potatoes are cut into, it can be enhanced by the addition of garlic or prosciutto, and you can even opt for soft or crispy skins. When cold, it makes an excellent basis for potato salad.

extra virgin olive oil

6 potatoes, peeled and cut into wedges

6 cm (2 in) sprig fresh rosemary, stem discarded

roughly ground salt, or Maldon sea salt

1 Preheat oven to 150°C (300°F), or 180°C (350°F) for crisper skins.

2 Into an ovenproof baking dish pour enough olive oil to coat the bottom thickly. Add the potato pieces and turn them over several times to coat with the oil. Sprinkle with the rosemary leaves.

3 Bake in the oven, uncovered, for 30 minutes. Turn potatoes and sprinkle generously with salt. Bake a further 30 minutes.

SERVES 4

≈ **TOMATOES (POMODORI)**

Canned plum (San Marzano) tomatoes are recommended in recipes requiring canned tomatoes, and those from Italy are hard to beat as they are sweet, full of colour and flavour, and they are tinned in thick, natural purée which can be used elsewhere.

FRIED PLUM TOMATOES

Plum tomatoes are ideal for this treatment as they are very fleshy and will keep intact.

8 fresh plum (San Marzano) tomatoes, not too ripe

salt and freshly ground black pepper

¼ cup (60 ml/4 fl oz) extra virgin olive oil

1 tablespoon chopped fresh basil

4 tablespoons grated Parmesan cheese

1 Cut each tomato in half along its length, then slice off some flesh on the rounded side to give two flat surfaces. Salt and pepper both sides.

2 Heat oil in a frying pan, add tomato slices and sprinkle on half the basil. Fry 1 minute and turn. Top slices with remaining basil and cook an extra minute.

3 Increase heat. Sprinkle half the Parmesan cheese over each slice, flip over and briefly fry. Repeat on other side with remaining Parmesan. Serve immediately.

SERVES 4

CREAMY BAKED POLENTA

4 cups (1 litre/32 fl oz) milk

60 g (2 oz) butter

1 teaspoon salt

1 cup (180 g/6 oz) fine polenta (instant polenta is good)

½ cup (60 g/2 oz) grated Emmenthal or Jarlsberg cheese

2 tablespoons grated Parmesan cheese

3 eggs, beaten

nutmeg

1 Preheat oven to 200°C (380°F) and grease a shallow ovenproof dish.

2 Put milk, butter and salt into a large saucepan and heat until almost boiling and butter has melted.

3 Add polenta and cook, stirring, until thick and smooth and mixture begins to come away from the sides of the pan.

4 Remove from heat and stir in cheeses. When these have melted, beat in eggs and season with nutmeg.

5 Transfer polenta into prepared dish, roughly levelling the surface.

6 Bake for 30 minutes or until top is golden. Cut into wedges and serve.

SERVES 4 TO 6

TUSCAN BEANS

350 g (11 oz) dried cannellini beans, soaked for at least 12 hours

5 to 6 fresh sage leaves

4 tablespoons olive oil

2 cloves garlic

500 g (1 lb) fresh tomatoes, peeled, seeded and chopped

salt and freshly ground black pepper

100 g (3½ oz) shelled broad beans

1 Drain cannellini beans, put in a saucepan with half the sage, 1 tablespoon of oil and cover with cold water. Bring to the boil and simmer until beans are tender, about 1 hour. Drain.

2 Heat remaining oil in a deep-sided frying pan and add the rest of the sage with the garlic. Over a low heat, lightly toss to combine flavours. Add tomatoes and drained beans, season with salt and pepper and cover pan. Simmer for 15 to 20 minutes. Add broad beans and simmer a further 10 minutes. Taste for salt and pepper. Serve hot or cold as an accompaniment to a meat course, or by itself with crusty bread.

SERVES 4 TO 6

Creamy Baked Polenta; Tuscan Beans

≈ TUSCAN BEANS

Tuscans love their beans, which are often served as a course on their own. This colourful version of Fagioli all'uccelletto also makes a very good accompaniment to meat dishes.

*he perfect way to
*ftover risotto or
boiled rice. In fact it
originated for just that
purpose, when the
remains of Risotto
Milanese, with its
saffron flavouring, was
too delicious and too
expensive to throw out!
If you are using boiled or
steamed rice, soak it in a
little milk before
proceeding to give a moist
consistency, and why not
flavour this with a pinch
of saffron?*

RICE PANCAKE

300 g (10 oz) leftover risotto or boiled rice

1 egg, beaten

1 to 2 tablespoons finely chopped fresh parsley (optional)

60 g (2 oz) mozzarella cheese, cut into small dice

2 tablespoons grated Parmesan cheese

2 tablespoons olive oil

grated Parmesan cheese, to serve

1 Put rice, egg, parsley, mozzarella and Parmesan in a bowl and toss lightly.

2 Heat oil in a solid based frying pan and add rice mixture. Flatten it out to about 1 cm (½ in) thick. Cook over a moderate heat until bottom is golden, moving it around in the pan once it starts to brown to prevent sticking. Place the pan lid or a large plate over the frying pan and quickly flip. Return to pan and cook until golden on the other side.

3 Slide onto a plate, cut into wedges and serve with extra grated Parmesan.

SERVES 4 TO 6

SARDINIAN FRITTATA

Halfway between a soufflé and an omelette, this style of frittata is basic and easy and can be made with just about any vegetable in season.

2 to 3 tablespoons olive oil

2 cloves garlic, finely chopped

2 teaspoons finely chopped fresh thyme or basil

1 tablespoon finely chopped fresh parsley

450 g (14 oz) young zucchini (courgettes), trimmed and sliced

4 eggs

1 slice (about 25 g) wholemeal bread, crusts discarded and soaked in 2 tablespoons milk

2 tablespoons grated Pecorino cheese

salt and freshly ground black pepper

2 tablespoons pine nuts

1 Preheat oven to 190°C (375°F) and grease a square or rectangular baking dish.

2 Heat olive oil in a large frying pan and add garlic and herbs. Stir to coat with oil, then add zucchini. Sauté gently until just tender and starting to brown. Remove from heat and set to one side.

3 Beat eggs in a bowl with the bread/milk until smooth, then stir in Pecorino. Add zucchini and salt and pepper to taste. Pour mixture into prepared dish, sprinkle over the pine nuts and bake in the oven until set, about 30 minutes. Allow to cool slightly before cutting into slices and serving. This frittata is good served cold for a barbecue or picnic.

SERVES 4

GLAZED SWEET AND SOUR ONIONS

750 g (1 ½ lb) small white onions, peeled and trimmed

60 g (2 oz) butter

3 tablespoons sugar

⅓ cup (100 ml/4fl oz) white wine vinegar

salt and freshly ground black pepper

½ teaspoon balsamic vinegar mixed with 1 tablespoon water

1 Place onions in a bowl and cover with cold water for at least 30 minutes. Drain.

2 Melt butter in a deep-sided frying pan and stir in sugar. Gently cook, stirring, for 3 to 4 minutes. Stir in vinegar and add onions. Season to taste with salt and pepper, cover pan and cook over a moderate heat until onions are golden and cooked through. From time to time swirl them around in the pan, and check that they aren't drying up. Just before serving, add balsamic vinegar mixture and toss well.

SERVES 4

EGGPLANT, ZUCCHINI AND EGGS

An unusual and attractive dish to serve with roast poultry, lamb or veal.

600 g (1¼ lb) long, thin eggplants (aubergines), sliced

1 onion

⅓ cup (100 ml/3 fl oz) olive oil

⅓ cup (100 ml/3 fl oz) vegetable oil

400 g (13 oz) zucchini (courgettes), sliced

pinch salt

3 tomatoes, peeled, seeded and chopped

freshly ground black pepper

2 eggs, beaten

1 teaspoon finely chopped fresh oregano or marjoram

1 Place eggplants in a bowl and cover with cold water. Cut onion in half around its middle, then slice lengthways into wedges.

2 Heat olive and vegetable oils in a deep-sided frying pan and sauté onion over a moderate heat until soft. Stir in zucchini and salt.

3 Drain eggplant slices and squeeze dry. Add to pan and fry until they and the zucchini are golden. Add tomatoes and season with pepper. Cook over a low heat, stirring often, for 15 minutes or until vegetables are cooked but still holding their shape. There will be only a little moisture left in the pan.

4 When ready to serve, remove pan from heat and toss through the egg and oregano. There will be enough heat in the dish to thicken the eggs and form a creamy sauce. Serve immediately.

SERVES 6

FRIED FENNEL

4 cups (1 litre/32 fl oz) water

1½ cups (350 ml/12 fl oz) dry white wine

1 tablespoon white wine vinegar

2 bay leaves

1 clove garlic

1 teaspoon salt

4 fennel bulbs

3 tablespoons breadcrumbs

3 tablespoons grated Parmesan cheese

2 eggs, beaten

olive oil, for frying

1 Put water, wine, vinegar, bay leaves, garlic and salt into a large saucepan and bring to the boil.

2 Remove tough outer layers from fennel bulbs and trim off tops. Cut them down their length into ½ cm (¼ in) slices, discarding the rounded slices from the sides.

Each slice will be joined at the bottom and slightly fan out at the top. Place these into saucepan, return to the boil and simmer until just tender, about 10 minutes. Drain and dry fennel on paper towels. Open out the tops of each slice to form a rough fan shape.

3 Toss breadcrumbs and Parmesan together in a plate.

4 Working one at a time, dip fennel slices into egg, shake off excess, then toss each in breadcrumb mixture to coat all surfaces.

5 Heat a good amount of olive oil in a large frying pan. Fry fennel slices until crisp and golden on both sides. Drain on paper towels and serve immediately.

SERVES 4

≈ BABY ONIONS

Sweet and sour baby onions, Cipolline in Agrodolce, can be served hot as an accompaniment to roasted meats, or allowed to cool and presented as part of an antipasti selection.

≈ FRIED FENNEL

Fennel is a particularly versatile vegetable. The bulb can be served cooked, as in Finocchio Milanese (Fried Fennel), or in salads. Young, crisp bulbs are eaten raw in place of fruit at the end of a meal. The leaves and stalks are used in stuffings, and the seeds flavour anything from salamis to dried figs.

BRAISED LEEKS WITH THYME

4 leeks

20 g (⅔ oz) butter

1 tablespoon olive oil

1 onion, thinly sliced

2 tomatoes, peeled, seeded and finely chopped

salt and freshly ground black pepper

2 to 3 sprigs fresh thyme

⅓ cup (100 ml/3 fl oz) light chicken or vegetable stock

Braised Leeks with Thyme

1 Trim green tops of leeks and cut off the bases, leaving a small section of bulb so that the leek won't fall apart when cut. Cut in half lengthways.

2 Heat butter and oil in a large frying pan and gently sauté onion until soft. Add the leeks, turning them over once or twice. Stir in tomatoes, season with salt and pepper, and add thyme and stock. Simmer over a low heat, turning occasionally, until leeks are tender, about 40 minutes.

3 Arrange leeks on a warm serving dish and spoon on the sauce. Serve hot as an accompaniment to roast or baked meats.

SERVES 4

SALAD GREENS WITH GORGONZOLA DRESSING

Walnuts and Gorgonzola cheese have a special affinity and turn up together in many dishes. This salad makes a good accompaniment to grilled meats, but can also be served as a light first course. The dressing can be used on cooked vegetables such as green beans or broccoli.

60 g (2 oz) Gorgonzola or other creamy blue cheese

2 tablespoons white wine vinegar

3 tablespoons extra virgin olive oil

3 tablespoons cream

1 teaspoon chopped fresh tarragon, or ½ teaspoon dried

⅔ cup (30 g/1 oz) walnut halves, broken in half again if large

mixed lettuce and salad greens (called mesticanza**)**

1 Using a fork, mash Gorgonzola in a bowl. Gradually incorporate vinegar, and then the olive oil. When smooth, stir in cream and tarragon. Blend well.

2 Add walnuts to salad bowl, pour over dressing and toss lightly.

SERVES 4 TO 6

≈ GORGONZOLA CHEESE

A blue-veined cheese from Lombardy. When young, it is soft, sweet and creamy, and when mature, dryer, sharp and pungent. If unavailable, substitute half creamy blue such as Blue Castello, and half a matured like Danish Blue.

Salad Greens with Gorgonzola Dressing

PIEDMONT PEAS

750 g (1 ½ lb) young peas in the pod

1 ½ tablespoons olive oil

100 g (3 ½ oz) onion, very thinly sliced

60 g (2 oz) pancetta or bacon, finely chopped

1 tablespoon finely chopped fresh parsley

1 cup (250 ml/8 fl oz) light chicken stock

salt and freshly ground black pepper

1 Shell peas and cover with cold water for 30 minutes.

2 Heat oil in a pan and add onion, pancetta and parsley. Sauté gently until onions are soft, about 10 minutes. Drain peas and add to pan along with the stock. Increase heat, cover pan and cook for 5 minutes. Taste for salt and pepper and continue cooking until peas are tender, another 5 to 8 minutes. If there is excess liquid before serving, increase heat and cook without the lid until it evaporates. Serve at once.

SERVES 4 TO 6

BAKED MUSHROOMS AND POTATOES

½ cup (125 ml/8 fl oz) olive oil

1 clove garlic, minced

4 tablespoons finely chopped fresh parsley

½ tablespoon finely chopped fresh basil

3 tablespoons breadcrumbs

3 tablespoons grated Pecorino cheese

salt and freshly ground black pepper

800 g (1 ½ lb) potatoes, peeled

350 g (11 oz) button mushrooms, thickly sliced

1 Preheat oven to 180°C (350°F) and grease a 25 cm (10 in) round ovenproof dish.

2 Combine garlic, parsley, basil, breadcrumbs and Pecorino in a bowl, and season with salt and pepper.

3 Cut potatoes into slices ½ cm (¼ in) thick. Arrange half in a single overlapping layer on the bottom of the dish. Sprinkle with a little salt, then layer half the mushrooms on top. Spread half the herb mixture over this, then drizzle on 2 tablespoons of oil. Repeat layers, pouring the remainder of the oil over the final herb layer. Cover dish tightly with foil and transfer to the oven.

4 Bake for 50 minutes, remove foil and bake a further 10 minutes. Serve as an accompaniment to roast meats.

SERVES 6 TO 8

BROAD BEANS FROM ASSISI

2 kg (4 lb) fresh broad beans

2 tablespoons olive oil

20 g (⅔ oz) butter

1 onion, thinly sliced

1 clove garlic, minced

100 g (3 ½ oz) pancetta or bacon, cut into short, narrow strips

⅓ cup (100 ml/3 fl oz) (more if necessary) light chicken or vegetable stock

freshly ground black pepper

1 Shell beans and remove skins, putting them into a bowl of cold water as they are done.

2 Heat oil and butter in a pan, then gently sauté onion, garlic and pancetta until golden. Add beans and stir to coat.

3 Add 2 to 3 tablespoons of stock, season with pepper and gently cook until beans are tender. If neccessary, add a little more stock to keep beans moist. The beans will have very little liquid left by the time they are cooked. Adjust seasoning, transfer to a warm bowl and serve at once.

SERVES 4

ZUCCHINI AND MINT SALAD

This simple salad has a great flavour when served cold and it keeps well for 1 to 2 days. It can also be eaten hot as soon as it is made. Choose small, young zucchini.

400 g (14 oz) thin zucchini (courgettes)

1 teaspoon salt

1 garlic clove, finely chopped

4 tablespoons olive oil

juice 1 lemon

3 to 4 sprigs fresh mint

freshly ground black pepper

1 Top and tail zucchinis and cut into 6 to 8 cm (3 to 4 in) lengths.

2 Bring a large pot of water to the boil, add salt and zucchini and simmer until they are tender but firm. Drain, then toss with garlic, oil, lemon juice and mint, and flavour to taste with black pepper.

SERVES 4

FRIED CAULIFLOWER AND BROCCOLI

These vegetables go well together because, apart from the similar texture and cooking times, there is a pleasing colour and flavour contrast. This amount will be enough for 4 people if served as a course on its own, or for 6 as an accompaniment to a main dish. If it is to be served as a side dish, you might like to make the florets quite small.

600 g (1¼ lb) trimmed cauliflower

600 g (1¼ lb) trimmed broccoli

salt

¾ cup (100 g/3½ oz) plain (all-purpose) flour

1 x 60 g (2 oz) egg, beaten

1 cup (250 ml/8 fl oz) dry white wine

olive oil for frying

1 Bring a large saucepan of water to the boil and add cauliflower and broccoli, and a large pinch of salt. Cook over a moderate heat until *al dente*. Drain, cool, then cut into florets.

2 In the meantime, combine flour, egg and enough wine to make a smooth batter. Season with salt and set aside to rest.

3 Heat enough oil in a saucepan to cover 5 to 6 florets at a time. Dip florets in the batter, shake off excess and fry, a few at a time, when oil is very hot. Drain on paper towels and serve at once.

SERVES 4

BROAD BEAN, SALAMI AND CHEESE SALAD

A taste for eating raw broad beans first began in Rome where the young new beans of early spring are particularly succulent. This salad has a good combination of flavours, textures and colour which makes it ideal for a buffet or picnic dish, and it can sit out for a number of hours without failing.

2 kg (4 lb) young fresh broad beans

1 red onion, thinly sliced

90 g (3 oz) salami of choice, cut into short thin strips

90 g (3 oz) Parmesan cheese in a block

2 hard-boiled eggs, finely chopped

salt and freshly ground black pepper

extra virgin olive oil

1 Shell beans and remove skins. Put in a bowl and toss with onion and salami. Shave Parmesan or cut into thin strips, then add to bowl. Add eggs, and salt and pepper to taste. Toss lightly with a little oil. Before serving, add more oil to taste.

SERVES 6 TO 8

CIAMMOTTA

250 g (8 oz) eggplant (aubergine), trimmed
and thinly sliced

salt

4 to 6 tablespoons olive oil

250 g (8 oz) potatoes, peeled and cubed

1 small green capsicum (pepper), trimmed
and thinly sliced

1 small red capsicum (pepper), trimmed and
thinly sliced

200 g (6½ oz) tomatoes, peeled, seeded and
chopped

1 clove garlic, minced

chopped fresh parsley, to garnish

extra virgin olive oil, optional

antipasti table or served
as an accompaniment to a
meat course. It can be
eaten warm or straight
from the refrigerator.

Ciammotta

1 Put eggplant in a colander and liberally sprinkle with salt. Let sit for 30 minutes to extract the juices. Lightly squeeze dry.

2 Heat 4 tablespoons of oil in a frying pan and brown potato, but do not cook through. Transfer to a heatproof casserole. Next fry the capsicum, and then the eggplant, adding them to the casserole as they begin to brown. If neccessary, add more oil as you go.

3 Toss through tomatoes, garlic and salt to taste. Put over a moderate heat and simmer, partially covered, for about 1 hour.

La ciammotta will be quite dry when done. Allow to cool. Serve with a sprinkling of chopped parsley, and drizzle over some oil.

SERVES 4

CAPSICUM AND MUSHROOM CASSEROLE

4 tablespoons olive oil

2 onions, thinly sliced

1 clove garlic, minced

1 tablespoon finely chopped fresh basil

1 tablespoon finely chopped fresh parsley

4 capsicum (peppers) of different colours, cut into 4 cm (1½ in) wedges

1 zucchini (courgette), sliced

150 g (5 oz) cap mushrooms, thickly sliced

2 tablespoons chicken or vegetable stock

3 tablespoons white wine vinegar

salt and freshly ground black pepper

2 potatoes, sliced

1 Heat oil in a heatproof casserole and add onions, garlic, basil, and parsley. Sauté over a moderate heat until onions are softened, about 12 minutes. Add capsicum, zucchini and mushrooms, toss, then stir in stock and vinegar. Season to taste. Cover pot tightly and cook over a low heat for 15 minutes.

2 Put potatoes in a layer on top, season lightly with salt and pepper and cover. Cook a further 15 to 20 minutes, or until capsicum are tender but still crisp. The potatoes will form a rough cover for the dish, but some will probably sink in.

SERVES 4 TO 6

*Capsicum and Mushroom
Casserole*

BROCCOLI AND PINE NUTS

500 g (1 lb) broccoli

salt

20 g (⅔ oz) butter

1 teaspoon very finely chopped onion

⅓ cup (100 ml/3 fl oz) cream

1 egg yolk

1 tablespoon finely chopped fresh parsley

freshly grated Parmesan cheese

pepper

2 tablespoons toasted pine nuts

1 Trim broccoli and cut into large florets keeping some stalk attached. Cook in a large pot of boiling salted water until tender but still crisp.

2 Melt butter in the top of a double boiler and add onion. Heat over gently simmering water for 5 minutes. Add cream, then beat in egg yolk. Cook, stirring occasionally, until sauce begins to thicken. Stir in parsley and some Parmesan, and season lightly with salt and pepper. If sauce is still a little thin, continue to cook.

3 When broccoli is cooked, drain and transfer to a warmed serving dish. Spoon sauce over the top, and toss through pine nuts. Serve hot.

SERVES 4

SALMORIGLIO

Originating in Sicily where it was mainly served with grilled swordfish, this sauce makes a great salad dressing. It goes particularly well with fresh cooked tuna which is then served as a seafood salad or an antipasti dish.

⅔ cup (150 ml/5 fl oz) extra virgin olive oil

4 tablespoons hot water

3 tablespoons fresh lemon juice

2 cloves garlic, finely chopped

1 teaspoon finely chopped fresh oregano, or ½ teaspoon dried

3 tablespoons finely chopped fresh parsley

1 Put olive oil in a bowl and gradually beat in water. Beat in lemon juice, then add garlic, oregano and parsley and beat well to combine. Place bowl over a saucepan of simmering water and cook, stirring, for 5 minutes. Bring to room temperature before using. To keep, refrigerate in an airtight jar.

MAKES ABOUT 1 ½ CUPS (350 ML/12 FL OZ)

SUMMER SALAD WITH ROASTED GARLIC DRESSING

DRESSING

4 large unpeeled cloves garlic

olive oil

1 tablespoon balsamic vinegar

⅓ cup (100 ml/3 fl oz) extra virgin olive oil

SALAD

200 g (6 ½ oz) very small button mushrooms, wiped clean

1 punnet cherry tomatoes, cut in half

150 g (5 oz) green beans, cut into 3 cm (1 ½ in) lengths and blanched

1 tablespoon shredded basil leaves

salt and freshly ground black pepper

1 Preheat oven to 180°C (350°F).

2 Put garlic in a small baking or pie dish and drizzle a little olive oil on top. Stir to coat. Place in the oven and roast until very soft, about 25 minutes. Cool. Open top end of each clove and squeeze pulp into a bowl. Blend with balsamic vinegar, then gradually mix in extra virgin olive oil.

3 Combine mushrooms, tomatoes and beans in a bowl. Add dressing and basil and toss lightly. Season to taste with salt and pepper, then set aside for at least 15 minutes before serving.

SERVES 4 TO 6

POTATO, ONION AND CHEESE PIE

A crustless pie which is formed in the manner of a lasagne, this is certainly not for the weight conscious! However it is easy, very satisfying and uses ingredients which are always present in the kitchen cupboard.

3 tablespoons breadcrumbs

700 g (1 lb 6 oz) large potatoes

salt

2 tablespoons light olive oil

90 g (3 oz) butter

750 g (1½ lb) onions, sliced

350 g (11 oz) thinly sliced prosciutto or ham

300 g (10 oz) Fontina or other melting cheese, in thin slices

100 g (3½ oz) grated Parmesan cheese

4 tablespoons finely chopped fresh parsley

1 Preheat the oven to 200°C (400°F). Grease a 24 cm (9½ in) springform pan and sprinkle in breadcrumbs to coat the bottom and sides.

2 Put potatoes and a good pinch of salt into a pot of boiling water and simmer until just cooked through. Drain and cool, then cut each one into slices. Set aside.

3 Melt olive oil and half the butter in a frying pan and gently sauté onions until soft.

4 Put a layer of proscuitto on the bottom of the prepared pan. Cover with a layer of onion, then a layer of potato slices. Next a layer of Fontina, then a sprinkling of Parmesan and parsley. Repeat layers in this manner until the ingredients are used up, finishing with the cheeses on top. Dot the surface with remaining butter. Transfer pan to oven and bake for 30 minutes, or until the cheeses are melted and golden.

5 Remove from the oven and cool for 10 to 15 minutes before unmoulding. Serve warm or at room temperature with a plain green or tomato salad.

SERVES 6

FRESH SALMON AND LEEK 'LASAGNE'

½ fennel bulb, about 150 g (5 oz)

2 leeks, white part only

90 g (3 oz) butter

½ cup (125 ml/4 fl oz) water

salt and white pepper

3 tablespoons cream

12 thin slices boneless fresh salmon fillets of 8 to 10 cm (3 to 4 in) square

1 Preheat oven to 200°C (400°F).

2 Trim fennel, reserving green tops, and remove tough outer leaves. Slice thinly. Trim leek, remove outer skin and slice thinly.

3 Heat three-quarters of the butter in a saucepan and add fennel and leek slices. Gently cook for 5 minutes. Add water and salt and pepper to taste. Cook a further 10 to 15 minutes, or until vegetables have softened and a thickish sauce is formed. Check seasoning, then strain off the liquid from the vegetables. Keep these to one side and put liquid in a small saucepan with cream. Bring to the boil and thicken slightly; there will only be 5 to 6 tablespoons.

4 In the meantime, trim salmon into uniform rounds and salt and pepper lightly. Chop fennel greens.

5 In a greased, shallow, ovenproof dish arrange 4 salmon slices just touching (to help support each other) and divide half the leek/fennel slices over each piece. Cover each with another slice of salmon, the remaining vegetables and lastly, the final slice of salmon. Stir fennel greens through remaining sauce and spoon over the top. Dot each 'lasagne' with the last of the butter, then transfer to the oven. Bake, uncovered, for 8 to 10 minutes or until salmon is just tender. Serve at once.

SERVES 4

≈ FRESH SALMON AND LEEK 'LASAGNE'

Of course this is not a totally vegetable recipe, but the role that the fennel and leeks play in the dish decided its inclusion here. For a strictly vegetarian dish, substitute tomato lasagne pasta for the salmon.

SWEETS

Many of the more famous Italian deserts, such as cassata, zabaione and cannoli originated in Sicily. Granita and sorbets have also featured in Sicilian menus for hundreds of years and marzipan fruits are another speciality.

Not all of Italy shares the Sicilian passion for sweets, though biscuits in one form or another often appear at the end of a meal. Pastries are important, particularly in southern regions such as Calabria and Campania, where elaborate creations are bought from the pasticceria for special occasions, leaving the simpler baking for the home cook.

Fresh fruit is a common final touch to a meal. In areas bordered by the Austrian Alps, such as in Alto Adige, potatoes are even included in sweets and cakes, and strudel and doughnuts are common desserts, along with puddings and tarts. Cheese is such an intrinsic part of Italian cuisine that recipes including ricotta or mascarpone frequently crop up on the dessert menu. Many people associate Italy with chocolate too, and amongst the recipes here, you'll find one especially for chocolate lovers!

Sugared Noodles with Citrus Sauce (page 86); Granita di Caffe (page 86); Blueberry and Mascarpone Tarts (page 83)

≈ **STYLISH APRICOTS**

This simple dessert, Grilled Stuffed Apricots, gives style to what is basically fresh fruit and cheese. If apricot kernel paste is available, do try it; it gives a subtle and interesting flavour.

GRILLED STUFFED APRICOTS

4 large ripe apricots

20 g (²⁄₃ oz) butter, room temperature

4 tablespoons icing sugar

2 tablespoons ground almonds

¹⁄₃ cup (80 g/3 oz) ricotta

½ teaspoon grated lemon rind

1 teaspoon ground ginger (optional)

1 teaspoon apricot kernel paste (optional)

1 Skin, stone and halve the apricots.

2 Grease a heatproof shallow dish with butter and place in the apricots, cut side up.

3 Turn the grill on to medium heat.

4 Sieve icing sugar into a small bowl and add ground almonds, ricotta and lemon rind. Combine well. Stir in ginger and apricot kernel paste, if used. Pile mixture into apricot halves.

5 Place under the grill 10 to 12 cm (4 to 5 in) from heat and cook 5 minutes.

6 Serve straight away, or cool to room temperature.

SERVES 4

≈ **PEACHES AND NECTARINES**

Nectarines with Zabaione and Hazelnuts great and doesn't require the fruit to be cooked. Big, ripe peaches work equally as well.

NECTARINES WITH ZABAIONE AND HAZELNUTS

4 large, ripe but firm yellow nectarines

²⁄₃ cup (150 ml/5 fl oz) good quality Marsala or semi-sweet sherry

3 egg yolks

¹⁄₄ cup (60 g/2 oz) caster sugar

finely grated zest of ½ lemon

²⁄₃ cup (150 ml/5 fl oz) cream, whipped

1 ½ tablespoons chopped candied peel

1 ½ tablespoons chopped roasted hazelnuts (filberts)

1 Peel nectarines and prick all over with a fine skewer. Put in a bowl and pour over half the Marsala. Cover and chill for 30 minutes. Drain off Marsala and add to the other half, and return nectarines to refrigerator.

2 In the top part of a double boiler, but not over heat, whisk egg yolks, sugar and lemon zest. Continue to whisk until sauce is thick and creamy. Gradually whisk in Marsala. Place over double boiler of gently simmering water and cook, stirring continually, until sauce is thick enough to coat the back of a spoon. Remove from heat but continue stirring until the sauce cools. Fold in whipped cream.

3 Spoon sauce over nectarines and chill for a further 1 hour. Before serving, pile the peel and nuts on top.

SERVES 4

GRANITA DI MELONE

½ cup (125 g/4 oz) sugar

²⁄₃ cup (150 ml/5 floz) water

750 g (1 ½ lb) ripe, peeled and cleaned rockmelon (cantaloup)

juice of ½ small lemon

1 Place sugar and water into a small pan and gently heat until the sugar dissolves. Increase heat and bring to the boil, then boil for 5 minutes. Remove and set aside to cool completely.

2 Cut melon into small pieces and purée in a processor, blender or mouli. Stir through lemon juice, then the cold sugar syrup. Pour into a shallow freezer tray and freeze for 30 minutes. Remove and whisk well for a minute or two. Return to freezer for 1 hour, mash up with the whisk once more, then freeze again 1 hour.

3 Transfer tray to the refrigerator 30 minutes before serving. When ready to serve, whisk up granita well to give a fine mushy ice, but one which still holds form. Serve immediately in tall sundae or parfait glasses.

SERVES 4

Nectarines with Zabaione and Hazelnuts

over the coun... ...so in the Veneto claims it as their own; certainly their version is much more elegant than some, and it is always made with mascarpone cheese. In other regions it resembles a bowl of trifle and is similar to Zuppa Inglese, so-called because the English visiting Italy, identifying with their trifle, became partial to it.

≈ **SAVOIARDI BISCUITS**

These are flattish sponge biscuits about 10 cm (4 in) long and are rarely made at home these days. They are also known as lady fingers.

TIRAMISU

3 egg yolks

¾ cup (185 g/6 oz) caster sugar

500 g (1 lb) mascarpone, or spreadable Philadelphia Cream Cheese

1 to 2 tablespoons rum

⅔ cup (200 ml/7 fl oz) very very very strong black coffee flavoured with 1 tablespoon sugar, then cooled

16 savoiardi biscuits (sponge fingers)

100 g (3½ oz) bitter chocolate cocoa, sifted

1 Using a wooden spoon beat egg yolks and sugar until smooth and creamy. Gently fold in mascarpone, then add rum to taste.

2 Pour coffee into a flat dish and, working one at a time, quickly soak the biscuits for about 5 seconds on each side.

3 On a flat base place 8 soaked biscuits in a row, side by side.

4 Spread half of mascarpone cream over these in a smooth layer. Grate over some chocolate, then a sprinkling of cocoa.

5 Follow with another level of coffee-infused biscuits, then spread on the remaining mascarpone. Grate the remaining chocolate on the top, and sprinkle over a little more cocoa.

6 Refrigerate for at least 4 hours or overnight. Transfer to a flat oblong plate and serve immediately in thin slices, unaccompanied.

SERVES 6 TO 8

MASCARPONE TART

PASTRY CASE

1½ cups (185 g/6 oz) plain (all-purpose) flour

pinch salt

100 g (3½ oz) butter, cut into pieces

2 tablespoons caster sugar

1 tablespoon grated lemon rind

1 egg yolk

1 to 2 tablespoons cold water

FILLING

375 g (12 oz) mascarpone, or sour cream

¾ cup (165 g/5½ oz) caster sugar

2 tablespoons cornflour

3 egg yolks, lightly beaten

1 teaspoon vanilla essence

2 tablespoons pine nuts, lightly toasted

1 TO PREPARE PASTRY CASE: (This step can be done in a food processor.) Sift flour and salt into a mixing bowl. Add butter and rub lightly into flour with your fingertips until mix resembles fine breadcrumbs. Stir through sugar. Add egg yolk, lemon rind and enough water to mix to a slightly crumbly, stiff dough.

Knead lightly, then cover with plastic wrap and chill for at least 1 hour.

2 Preheat oven to 180°C (350°F) and grease an 18 cm (7 in) loose-bottomed low-sided pie pan.

3 Roll out pastry and line pan. Neaten top edge, and prick base with a fork. Line with greaseproof paper and cover bottom with dried beans or peas. Bake for 10 minutes, then remove paper and beans and return to oven for another 5 minutes, or until golden. Remove from oven and cool before use.

4 TO PREPARE FILLING: Heat mascarpone in top bowl of a double boiler. When it is warm and runny, add sugar and cornflour. Stir in egg yolks, blend well and cook over a gentle heat until smooth and thick, at least 20 minutes. Stir from time to time. Remove from heat and cool for 20 minutes before stirring in vanilla essence.

5 Spoon into prepared pastry case, levelling surface with the back of the spoon. Sprinkle pine nuts around the outer rim, and chill before serving.

SERVES 4

RICOTTA FRITTA

Fried ricotta fritters are a specialty of the southern regions of Apulia and Basilicata. Sometimes dry ricotta is just cut into slices, dipped in flour and egg and deep-fried; in other places, as with this recipe, the ricotta is flavoured first. The fritters can be eaten as is, sprinkled with icing or caster sugar, or served with a drizzle of lemon juice.

100 g (3½ oz) ricotta cheese

⅓ cup (90 g/3 oz) sugar

salt

⅔ cup (100 g/3½ oz) plain (all-purpose) flour

5 eggs

1¼ cups (300 ml/10 fl oz) cream

¾ cup (200 ml/7 fl oz) milk

grated rind of 1 lemon

pinch nutmeg

vegetable oil

small handful semolina

1 Mash or sieve ricotta into a bowl. Stir in sugar, a pinch of salt and flour. Add eggs, one at a time, to form a smooth mixture, then whisk in cream, milk and lemon rind. Season with nutmeg.

2 Transfer mixture to a saucepan and heat, whisking constantly, until thickened. Remove from heat just as it reaches boiling point.

3 With some of the oil, grease a rectangular pan or dish big enough to hold the mixture at about 1 cm (½ in) thick. Pour in ricotta batter and level off the top. Leave to cool and set.

4 Cut into diamond shapes and coat each side lightly with semolina.

5 Heat 1 to 2 cm (½ to ¾ in) oil in a large frying pan and gently fry diamonds, a few at a time, until golden all over. Drain on paper towels before serving.

SERVES 4 TO 6

BLUEBERRY AND MASCARPONE TARTS

These delicious little dessert tarts combine fresh blueberries, balsamic vinegar and a crisp pastry made with olive oil.

PASTRY

1½ cups (185 g/6 oz) plain (all-purpose) flour

2 tablespoons sugar

1 teaspoon grated lemon zest

large pinch salt

3 tablespoons light olive oil

2 to 3 tablespoons milk

TOPPING

300 g (10 oz) blueberries

1½ tablespoons icing sugar

1 teaspoon balsamic vinegar

300 g (10 oz) mascarpone cheese

icing sugar for dusting

1 Preheat oven to 200°C (400°F) and grease a baking tray.

2 **TO PREPARE PASTRY:** Stir flour, sugar, lemon zest and salt with a fork until well mixed. Whisk the oil and 2 tablespoons milk together, then gradually blend into flour mixture with the fork. Keep working until a dough forms, adding more milk if neccessary. Divide dough into sections, then roll each one out to 5 mm (¼ in) thickness. Using a fluted cookie cutter of 6 to 7 cm (2½ in) diameter, cut out 12 circles and transfer them to the baking tray as you work. With the scraps of dough, cut out little leaf shapes and place on baking tray between the circles. Bake in the oven until golden, 10 to 12 minutes. Cool.

3 Meanwhile, combine blueberries, sugar and balsamic vinegar and set aside.

4 When ready to serve, put a dollop of mascarpone on each pastry base and pile some blueberries on top. Garnish with pastry leaves and sprinkle with icing sugar.

MAKES 12 TARTS

*Attractive when made as
either small individual
tarts or into one large pie,
this rich, not too sweet,
filling keeps very well
and can be served as a
dessert or with a cup of
coffee for afternoon tea.*

*After Christmas or
Easter we often find
ourselves with leftover
panettone or Colomba.
Here is a delicious way,
called Dolce di Pere, to
use them up, courtesy of
the thrifty housewives of
Alto Adige.*

ALMOND AND PINE NUT TART

PASTRY

1 cup (125 g/4 oz) plain (all-purpose) flour

100 g (3½ oz) butter, chilled and cut into
pieces

2 tablespoons caster sugar

1 egg, lightly beaten

FILLING

220 g (7 oz) almond paste, cut into small
pieces

90 g (3 oz) butter, softened

⅓ cup (80 g/2½ oz) caster sugar

1 teaspoon almond flavoured liqueur,
optional

4 eggs

¼ cup (30 g/1 oz) plain flour

½ teaspoon baking powder

4 tablespoons pine nuts

apricot jam

1 Preheat oven to 200°C (400°F) and grease
a 23 cm (9 in) loose-based pan.

2 TO PREPARE PASTRY: (This step can be
done in a processor.) Place flour in a bowl
and cut in butter and sugar. When mixture
resembles fine breadcrumbs, incorporate the
egg. Knead lightly until smooth, then form
dough into a ball. Wrap in foil or plastic
wrap and chill for at least 30 minutes.

3 TO PREPARE FILLING: (This step can also
be done in a processor.) Beat almond paste,
butter, sugar and liqueur together. When
mixture is smooth, beat in eggs, one at a
time, mixing well after each addition. Add
flour and baking powder and continue to
beat mixture until smooth.

4 Roll dough out into a circle 2 to 3 mm
(⅛ in) thick. Fit it into prepared pan and
trim the top edge.

5 Gently melt a little apricot jam and when
warm, paint it over the pastry surface. Add
almond filling, smooth the top and evenly
distribute the pine nuts over the surface.

Bake for 10 minutes. Reduce temperature to
190°C (375°F) and bake a further 10
minutes, or until tart is golden and set.

Serve at room temperature. If serving as a
dessert, accompany tart with whipped cream
or softened vanilla ice cream.

SERVES 6 TO 8

PANETTONE PUDDING

2 cups (500 ml/16 fl oz) red wine

⅓ cup (90 g/3 oz) caster sugar

500 g (1 lb) firm but ripe pears

juice ½ lemon

160 g (5 oz) butter

10 to 12 thin slices panettone, Colomba or
stale bread

¾ cup (90 g/3 oz) slivered almonds

½ cup (90 g/3 oz) sultanas (optional)

cream, for serving

1 Preheat oven to 180°C (350°F) and grease
a deep-sided ovenproof dish.

2 Combine wine and sugar and set aside.
Peel, core and slice pears, sprinkling the cut
surfaces with lemon juice as you work.

3 Lightly butter panettone slices on both
sides using half the butter. Place on a baking
tray and bake until lightly toasted.

4 Form a layer of toasts on the bottom of
the prepared dish. Sprinkle liberally with
sweetened wine, then cover with a layer of
pear slices. Top with a few almonds and
sultanas and dot with butter. Repeat layers
until all the ingredients are used up,
distributing the last of the butter on top.

5 Transfer to the oven and bake for
30 minutes. Serve warm, accompanied
with cream.

SERVES 6 TO 8

*Almond and Pine Nut Tart (back);
Panettone Pudding (front)*

GRANITA DI CAFFE

Granita is the perfect summer dessert as it is light, not too sweet and very refreshing. It is ideal to make at home because no special equipment is needed for good results, as with icecream or gelato, and anyway, it can't be bought and taken home! What could be more suitable on a steamy summer's evening than a slightly bitter coffee granita, made from freshly ground quality beans.

GRANITA DI CAFFE

2 cups (500 ml/16 fl oz) freshly made strong espresso

⅓ cup (90 g/3 oz) caster sugar

1 When the coffee is just made, transfer to a bowl and add sugar. Mix well to dissolve then transfer to a flat ice-cube tray or lamington tray and set aside. When cool, cover with plastic wrap and freeze for 30 minutes. Remove and stir mixture with a whisk, scraping down the sides of the tray. Return to freezer for 1 hour. Once again stir the mixture with a whisk, breaking it up. Return to freezer for 1 more hour.

2 About 10 minutes before serving, transfer tray to the refrigerator. Then when ready to eat, whisk or chop the granita into fine particles of mushy ice. Spoon into chilled long glasses and serve immediately, topped with lightly sweetened whipped cream and a sprinkling of powdered chocolate.

SERVES 4 TO 6

ROMAN CHEESECAKE

This baked ricotta cake has no crust and is surprisingly light. Two tablespoons of dried or crystallised fruit such as cherries or mixed peel may be added.

3 tablespoons sultanas

2 tablespoons Marsala or rum

plain (all-purpose) flour for dusting

1¾ cups (450 g/15 oz) ricotta cheese

100 g (3½ oz) sour cream

4 tablespoons wholemeal flour

4 tablespoons honey

1 teaspoon vanilla essence

3 eggs, separated

2 tablespoons grated lemon rind

1 Add sultanas to Marsala and set aside for at least 1 hour.

2 Preheat oven to 180°C (350°F). Grease an 18 cm (7 in) springform pan and dust it with flour.

3 Combine ricotta, sour cream, wholemeal flour, honey, vanilla and egg yolks in a bowl and mix well. Stir through sultanas, Marsala and lemon rind. Beat the egg whites until stiff and fold into ricotta mixture. Transfer to prepared pan and bake for about 45 minutes or until a skewer comes out clean from the centre. Remove from oven and cool before removing sides.

SERVES 6

SUGARED NOODLES WITH CITRUS SAUCE

This is in no way traditional, but sweet pasta dishes are establishing themselves as more than just a passing fad. They are light, easy to digest at the end of a meal, and elegant in their simplicity.

½ cup (125 g/4 oz) sugar

2 tablespoon fresh lemon juice

4 tablespoons fresh orange or tangerine juice

3 egg yolks

¼ teaspoon grated lemon rind

⅔ cup (150 ml/5 fl oz) cream

2½ tablespoons caster sugar

350 g (11 oz) fresh ribbon egg pasta, or 250 g (8 oz) dried e.g. linguine, fettuccine, taglierini

1 teaspoon butter

julienned orange peel, to garnish

small piece of chocolate, grated, to garnish

1 In a small saucepan, heat half the sugar with lemon and orange juices.

2 In a bowl, whisk the remaining sugar into the egg yolks until smooth and pale. Gradually whisk this into lemon syrup over a low heat. Add lemon rind and cook gently, stirring, until smooth and slightly thickened. Do not boil. Strain through a sieve.

3 Beat cream until stiff, then fold into the sauce. Return sauce to a saucepan and keep warm, but do not allow to boil.

4 Put a large pan of water on to boil, add 2 tablespoons caster sugar and boil pasta until *al dente*. Drain and toss with butter and remaining caster sugar.

5 Spoon a little sauce onto warmed plates, arrange pasta in a pile in the middle and spoon over remaining sauce. Top with orange peel and a few shavings of chocolate. Serve at once.

SERVES 4

BISQUIT TORTONI

A simple ice cream which only needs one freezing, this is a hit with children and adults alike. It can be put straight into the freezer in serving dishes, if desired.

40 g (1½ oz) sliced or flaked blanched almonds

½ tablespoon caster sugar

white of 1 large egg

1¼ cups (300 ml/10 fl oz) cream

4 tablespoons icing sugar

2 tablespoons brandy

1 tablespoon honey

1 Spread almonds over a baking tray, sprinkle with caster sugar and place under a moderate grill. Gently toast, tossing frequently, until the sugar has caramelised and the almonds lightly browned. Set aside to cool.

2 Beat the egg white until soft peaks form. In another bowl whisk cream until soft peaks form, then gradually whisk in the icing sugar, brandy and honey and continue whisking until thick. Gently fold in egg white.

3 Transfer mixture to a deep freezerproof tray to a depth of 4 to 5 cm (2 in), or divide between 6 to 8 individual moulds. Top with the toasted almonds and cover with foil.

Freeze until firm, at least 3 hours.

4 Transfer to the refrigerator 15 to 20 minutes before serving, to soften slightly. Scoop out servings from the tray, or unmould single serves and serve at once.

SERVES 6 TO 8

SWEET FOCACCIA

2 tablespoons sultanas

2 tablespoons warm water

1 teaspoon vanilla

280 g (9 oz) stale bread, rinds removed

8 eggs, separated

1 cup (220 g/7 oz) caster sugar

60 g (2 oz) candied fruit (try pawpaw or pineapple), finely chopped

grated rind of 1 lemon

pinch salt

icing sugar, for dusting

1 Preheat oven to 180°C (350°F) and grease a deep, wide cake pan.

2 Cover sultanas with water and vanilla and steep for 15 minutes.

3 Make breadcrumbs from the stale bread, as fine as possible. Put 2 tablespoons into prepared pan and coat the surface.

4 Whisk egg yolks and sugar together until pale and fluffy. Add remaining breadcrumbs in batches, mixing well but lightly after each addition. Gently stir in drained sultanas, candied fruit, lemon rind and salt.

5 Whisk egg whites until stiff, then very carefully fold them into the breadcrumb mixture. When evenly distributed, transfer mixture to prepared pan and bake for 45 minutes, or until golden. Remove from the oven, rest for 5 minutes then turn out of the pan. Serve when cool, dusted with icing sugar.

SERVES 10 TO 12

≈ **SWEET FOCACCIA**

A good all purpose flat cake originally from the Veneto which can be served for breakfast, with lunch, after the evening meal or in between any of these!

BACKGROUND FROM TERAZZO & CO. PTY LTD, PLATE FROM CYDONIA THE GLASS STUDIO

Ricotta and Apple Slice (page 90)

RICOTTA CREAM WITH GINGER AND FIGS

Ginger and spices, a legacy from the Greek Byzantine occupation, still turn up in the food of Basilicata. There figs, another favourite of the Greeks, are preserved and stored for use during the winter months. Fresh figs are also good in this recipe and if used, allow 1 large fig per person. The ginger may be omitted without jeopardising the appeal of the ricotta cream.

1 cup (250 g/8 oz) ricotta cheese

2 eggs, separated

¼ cup (55 g/2 oz) caster sugar

finely grated rind of 1 lemon

1 to 2 tablespoons finely chopped preserved or crystallised ginger

½ cup (125 ml/4 fl oz) cream

8 preserved figs; either dried or canned

small lemon leaves, to garnish (optional)

1 Sieve the ricotta, or put through a mouli. Add egg yolks and caster sugar and beat until smooth. Stir through lemon rind and add ginger to taste.

2 Whip cream just until soft peaks begin to form, then fold into ricotta mixture.

3 Whip egg whites until firm peaks hold and fold into mixture. This can be made up to 3 hours before serving.

4 Arrange figs, either sliced or whole, on dessert plates and serve with ricotta cream. Garnish with lemon leaves.

SERVES 4

Ricotta Cream with Ginger and Figs

≈ SWEET RICOTTA

Sweet pastries made with ricotta are common throughout Italy and often fresh fruit or jam are made into crostata. Here the two are combined to give an apple slice with a ricotta topping in a crostata crust.

RICOTTA AND APPLE SLICE

PASTRY

¾ cups (90 g/3 oz) self-raising flour

30 g (1 oz) butter

3 tablespoons caster sugar

1 ½ tablespoons fresh lemon juice

FILLING

5 tablespoons sultanas

1 tablespoons brandy

20 g (⅔ oz) butter

3 green cooking apples, peeled, cored and sliced

2 cups (500 g/1 lb) ricotta cheese

2 eggs, lightly beaten

½ cup (125 g/4 oz) caster sugar

2 tablespoons plain (all-purpose) flour

½ cup (125 ml) milk

2 teaspoons grated lemon rind

1 TO PREPARE PASTRY: (This step can be done in a processor.) Sift flour and cut butter into it. Stir through sugar, then add lemon juice and mix to a smooth dough. Knead lightly on a floured surface, wrap in foil or plastic wrap and chill for 30 minutes.

2 Preheat oven to 180°C (350°F) and grease a 23 cm (9 in) square cake pan.

3 TO PREPARE FILLING: First soak sultanas in brandy and set to one side. Melt butter in a frying pan and lightly sauté apple slices for 1 to 2 minutes. In a bowl, beat together ricotta, eggs, sugar, flour, milk and lemon rind.

4 Roll out dough to 3 mm (⅛ in) thickness and line the base of prepared pan. Arrange apples over pastry in pan. Stir sultanas through ricotta mix, then spread this over apples, smoothing the surface.

5 Bake for 1 hour, or until pastry is golden and filling set. Allow to cool before cutting into squares.

SERVES 8

≈ ZALETI

Zaleti, or Gialletti, are yellow cookies made with cornmeal, sultanas and pine nuts. They are found all over the Veneto where everyone seems to have their favourite recipe. Sometimes the dough is cut into diamonds, others prefer the traditional round cookie shape, and there is even a cake version called Zaletto.

ZALETI

½ cup (90 g /3 oz) sultanas

2 tablespoons brandy

1 cup (155 g/5 oz) cornmeal

1 ¼ cups (155 g/5 oz) plain (all-purpose) flour

½ teaspoon baking powder

pinch salt

155 g (5 oz) butter, softened

3 egg yolks

⅓ cup (90 g/3 oz) caster sugar

grated rind of 1 lemon

⅓ cup (40 g/1 ½ oz) pine nuts

½ teaspoon vanilla

1 Preheat oven to 190°C (375°F) and grease a baking tray.

2 Soak sultanas in brandy for at least 30 minutes. Squeeze off excess brandy and reserve sultanas.

3 Place cornmeal, flour, baking powder and salt in a large bowl and stir to combine. Work in butter until the mixture resembles breadcrumbs.

4 In another bowl beat egg yolks and sugar until smooth and pale. Work this into flours, and when a dough starts to form, add lemon rind, pine nuts, vanilla and reserved sultanas. Knead dough until smooth, adding a little milk or some extra flour to form a pliable texture.

5 Divide dough in half and roll each into a log of about 4 cm (1 ½ in) diameter. Cut into slices 1 cm (½ in) thick and position these at intervals on the prepared baking tray. Press each one in the middle to spread it out slightly. Bake until golden, 10 to 15 minutes. When cooled, they may be dusted with icing sugar.

MAKES ABOUT 30

SICILIAN CANNOLI

PASTRY CASES

2 cups (250 g/8 oz) plain (all-purpose) flour

pinch salt

2 teaspoons instant coffee

2 teaspoons cocoa

2 tablespoons caster sugar

60 g (2 oz) butter, cut into pieces

about 1 cup (250 ml/8 fl oz) Marsala

olive oil for frying

FILLING

1 cup (250 g/8 oz) ricotta

1½ cups (250 g/8 oz) icing sugar

4 teaspoons orange flower water

30 g (1 oz) dark chocolate, grated

60 g (2 oz) candied peel

icing sugar for dusting

1 TO PREPARE PASTRY: Stir together flour, salt, coffee, cocoa and sugar. Using a fork, work in butter until combined, then work in enough Marsala to make a firm dough. Knead lightly, then roll out into a thin sheet. Cut into 18 squares, 7½ cm x 7½ cm (2½ x 2½ in). Place metal cases diagonally across the squares and fold the corners across to overlap in the middle. Moisten overlapping dough, then press firmly to seal.

2 Deep-fry tubes, a few at a time, in hot oil deep enough to cover them. When golden and crisp, remove with a slotted spoon and leave to cool, still on their cases.

3 TO PREPARE FILLING: Beat together ricotta, icing sugar and orange flower water until smooth. Fold in chocolate and peel. Rest in the refrigerator until set.

4 Slide pastry tubes off cases. Using a piping bag or a spoon, stuff tubes with filling leaving some exposed at each end. Dust with extra icing sugar before serving. Cannoli don't keep beyond a couple of hours once they have been filled.

MAKES 18

TOZZETTI

These fat little biscuit bars from Venice have a rich and subtle flavour which belies their plain exterior.

125 g (4 oz) butter, room temperature

½ cup (125 g/4 oz) caster sugar

2 eggs and 1 egg yolk, beaten together

1 tablespoon fresh lemon juice

1 tablespoon fresh orange juice

1 teaspoon grated orange zest

1 teaspoon vanilla

2 cups (250 g/8 oz) plain (all-purpose) flour

¼ teaspoon salt

2 cups (250 g/8 oz) toasted and skinned hazelnuts (filberts), roughly chopped

2 tablespoons finely chopped candied orange peel

1 Preheat oven to 190°C (375°F). Grease a baking tray and dust it with flour.

2 Cream butter and sugar in a bowl until pale. Reserve 1 tablespoon of beaten egg, then add the remainder to butter. Beat well, then mix in lemon and orange juices, orange zest and vanilla. Add flour, salt, hazelnuts and peel and lightly fold in. If the dough feels too soft to roll out at this point, wrap it in plastic wrap or foil and refrigerate until firm, 1 to 1½ hours.

3 Roll out dough on a lightly floured surface to an even rectangle 36 x 25 cm (14 x 10 in). Roll dough over the rolling pin and transfer to the prepared baking tray. Brush the surface with reserved egg before transferring to the oven. Bake until glossy and blonde, but not golden (the centre should be a little soft), about 15 minutes.

4 Remove from oven and rest for 10 minutes. Cut into bars 10 x 4 cm (4 x 1½ in) while still warm, then transfer to racks to cool.

MAKES 20

≈ **SICILIAN CANNOLI**

One of Sicily's most famous sweets, cannoli are so very delicious, so light, that having a strong will is definitely vantaggioso! To make the cases, you will need the metal cylinders called cannelli which are available from kitchen shops. Dried, uncooked cannelloni tubes can also be used, but if all else fails, ready made cannoli cases can often be bought in Italian pastry shops or delicatessens.

Piatto di Cioccolate

PIATTO DI CIOCCOLATE

200 g (7 oz) dark cooking chocolate, cut into small pieces

100 g (3½ oz) butter

4 eggs, separated

3 tablespoons caster sugar

1 pinch baking powder

1 Preheat oven to 180°C (350°F). Grease a 25 cm (10 in) springform pan and dust it with flour.

2 Put chocolate and butter in the top of a double boiler and melt over a low heat. Remove from heat and cool.

3 Whip egg whites until soft peaks form.

4 Beat egg yolks with sugar until sugar is fully dissolved but the mixture remains a rich yolk colour. Gradually add cooled chocolate mixture to egg mixture and mix well. Lightly fold in egg whites. Transfer to prepared pan and bake for 30 minutes. Cool for 15 minutes before turning out. Serve at room temperature, sliced into wedges.

SERVES 8 TO 10

TORTA TANZINI

PASTRY

2¼ cups (280 g/9 oz) plain (all-purpose) flour

1 teaspoon baking powder

⅓ cup (90 g/3 oz) sugar

100 g (3½ oz) butter, cut into small cubes

1 egg yolk

grated rind of 1 lemon

FILLING

2¼ cups (200 g/6½ oz) roasted hazelnuts

white of 1 egg

⅓ cup (90 g/3 oz) sugar

1 teaspoon brandy

⅛ teaspoon almond essence

1 egg yolk, beaten

1 TO PREPARE PASTRY: (This step can be done in a food processor.) Mix flour, baking powder and sugar together. Cut butter through with a fork until a breadcrumb-like texture forms. Add egg yolk and lemon rind and mix, first with the fork and then by hand, until a smooth dough forms. Wrap in plastic wrap and chill for 1 hour.

2 Preheat oven to 180°C (350°F) and grease a baking tray.

3 TO PREPARE FILLING: Place hazelnuts, egg white, sugar, brandy and almond essence into processor. Process until a slightly coarse paste forms.

4 Remove pastry from the refrigerator and let sit at room temperature for 10 minutes.

On a floured surface, roll out to a large rectangle of 5 mm (¼ in) thickness. Spread the hazelnut filling over this.

5 From one of the widest sides roll pastry up, Swiss-roll fashion. Cut in half, trim the ends and place each roll on the prepared baking tray with the exposed edge underneath. Paint surfaces with egg yolk. Lightly make a lattice pattern on the top with a sharp knife being careful not to cut through the pastry. Bake for 30 minutes, or until golden.

6 Allow to cool before slicing. When ready to serve, cut slices about 1 cm (½ in) thick with a sharp knife.

BISCOTTONI

1 ¾ cups (220 g/7 oz) plain (all-purpose) flour
pinch salt
1 cup (220 g/7 oz) caster sugar

185 g (6 oz) butter
1 egg, beaten
60 g (2 oz) blanched almonds, toasted
60 g (2 oz) pine nuts, toasted
60 g (2 oz) pistachio kernels, toasted

1 Preheat oven to 180°C (350°F) and grease a 20 cm (8 in) round sandwich cake pan.
2 Sift flour and salt, then stir in sugar. Work in butter until a uniform mix forms, then add egg, reserving 1 teaspoon. Mix to give a smooth, crumbly biscuit dough. Add nuts and stir to distribute evenly.
3 Press mixture into prepared pan, smooth the surface and brush with reserved egg. Lightly press a knife onto the surface to indicate serving wedges, but don't press in too deeply.
4 Bake for 45 minutes or until golden. Cool in pan before turning out.

SERVES 8 PORTIONS

Torta Tanzini (right); Biscottoni (left)

≈ TORTA TANZINI

This pastry is very easy to handle when preparing and it has good keeping qualities. It cuts into attractive pinwheel slices which are just the thing for nibbling on with a cup of espresso or a glass of sweet wine.

This Sicilian loaf is wickedly rich, and with the help of a food processor, wickedly easy! It can be made a day or two in advance, and it freezes well provided that it goes into the freezer without the cream coating. The addition of ginger gives a subtle, clean tang but it may be omitted.

CHESTNUT LOAF

870 g (1¾ lb) canned chestnut purée

110 g (3½ oz) butter, melted

¾ cup (200 ml/7 fl oz) chocolate syrup

3 to 5 tablespoons Strega or Marsala

60 g (2 oz) preserved ginger, chopped into ½ to 1 cm (¼ to ½ in) pieces

1¼ cups (300 ml) cream

2 tablespoons icing sugar

¾ cup (100 g/3½ oz) pistachio kernels, toasted and coarsely chopped

1 Whip chestnut purée in a processor until softened. Add butter, chocolate syrup and 3 to 4 tablespoons of Strega and blend until smooth. Stir in ginger pieces.

2 Combine 1 tablespoon Strega and 2 tablespoons water. Lay out a large sheet of strong foil and liberally brush with Strega/water.

3 Transfer chestnut mixture to centre of foil and mould into a smooth and even thick log shape. Fold up foil to tightly encase the loaf, then refrigerate for at least 2 hours.

4 Whip cream with icing sugar until stiff. Unmould loaf onto a serving plate and spread with cream. Decorate the top with pistachios and chill until ready to serve. Cut into thin slices to serve.

SERVES 10 TO 12

SEMIFREDDO DI RICOTTA

4 eggs, separated

⅓ cup (90 g/3 oz) caster sugar

4 to 6 teaspoons rum

2 cups (500 g/1 lb) fresh ricotta cheese

1 Beat egg yolks with sugar in a bowl until smooth and pale. Stir in rum to taste. Force ricotta through a sieve and add to egg mixture. Combine well.

2 Whisk egg whites until firm peaks form. Lightly but thoroughly fold into ricotta mixture.

3 Line an oblong cake pan with foil, pressing it into the corners and smoothing out any creases. Spoon in ricotta mixture, then give the pan a good knock or two on the bench to release air bubbles. Smooth the surface and cover with a sheet of foil.

4 Freeze and until set, at least 2 hours. Just before serving, turn out of pan onto a serving platter and carefully peel off foil. Serve at once, accompanied by small dessert biscuits or slices of fresh fruit.

SERVES 4 TO 6

OVEN TEMPERATURES

TEMPERATURES	CELSIUS (°C)	FAHRENHEIT (°F)	GAS MARK
Very slow	120	250	½
Slow	150	300	2
Moderately slow	160-180	325-350	3-4
Moderate	190-200	375-400	5-6
Moderately hot	220-230	425-450	7
Hot	250-260	475-500	8-9

NOTE: We developed the recipes in this book in Australia where the tablespoon measure is 20 ml. In many other countries the tablespoon is 15 ml. For most recipes this difference will not be noticeable.

However, for recipes using baking powder, gelatine, bicarbonate of soda, small amounts of flour and cornflour, we suggest you add an extra teaspoon for each tablespoon specified.

GLOSSARY

Agrodolce Literally, sharp and sweet, the taste of sweet and sour aquired by flavouring dishes with sugar and wine vinegar. Also known as Saor in some regions such as the Veneto.

Al dente Literally 'to the tooth', describing the desirable state of pasta, rice, some vegetables etc when cooked; there should be resistence when bitten into and a firm, palpable texture.

Arborio rice A short, plump grained rice from the Po Valley. Arborio and Carnaroli are both superfine varieties which have the best qualities for making risotto. If unavailable, look for Violone (a semi-fine variety).

Balsamic Vinegar (*Aceto balsamico*) From Modena in Emilia-Romagna, this vinegar is made from the boiled down must of selected white grapes. It is aged in a series of different wood barrels to become concentrated, syrupy and aromatic. Use sparingly.

Bocconcini Small balls of fresh mozzarella cheese with a life of 4 to 5 days. If unavailable, don't substitute matured mozzarella, but other soft, fresh Italian cheeses, such as *stracchino* or *taleggio*.

Butter (Burro) Italian butter is always unsalted, and sometimes very creamy, as in *burro di panna* from Emilia-Romagna.

Dried tomatoes (*Pomodori secchi*) Sun-dried tomatoes are available in the dry state, or marinated in oil, often with garlic and herbs. They can be dark and concentrated in flavour, or lighter and plumper, with a more subtle taste. If buying them unmarinated, they will need to be soaked in warm water for at least 30 minutes before using.

Emmenthal cheese (*Emmenthaler*) Swiss cheese characterised by large holes and a golden yellow colour. Has a slightly nutty flavour and melts well while still maintaining form.

Fontina cheese A mild, slightly nutty cheese from the Piedmonte region which has good melting qualities.

Mascarpone Fresh cream cheese originally from Lombardy with a rich, slightly tangy flavour. Substitute half thick cream and half sour cream.

Mozzarella cheese A rindless cheese with good melting qualities originally made from buffalo milk. Now made from cow's milk it can be fresh, with 4 to 5 days life, or matured. When fresh it is white in colour and is eaten as a table cheese, whereas matured is a more golden colour and is used in cooking.

Olive oil, extra virgin Olive oil made from the first pressing of slightly under-ripe olives, and the better ones produced without chemical means. It has a low acidity (under 1 per cent by law) and no cholesterol.

Olive oil, light Has been developed by the big olive oil companies of Italy to give an oil which has a lighter olive flavour. It is ideal for cooking (even sweet baking), is a paler colour and is, like all other olive oils, without cholesterol. Look for the names Lite, Mild & Light or Extra Light on the label of your favourite brand.

Olive Paste (*Pâté di oliva*) Pulp of the olives made from either green or black olives.

Pancetta Unsmoked bacon which has been cured in spices, salt and pepper.

Pappardelle Wide flat ribbon pasta, usually 22 mm in width, which is traditionally served with sauces made from game or other wild things.

Parmesan cheese There are two types of Italian Parmesan: *Grana Pedano* or *Parmigiano Reggiano*. The latter is the best quality, being made only in a restricted area around Parma and under very strict regulations. It must be matured for at least 2 years and is sweet and moist when young, becoming dryer and sharper with age. It will have the words *Parmigiano Reggia*no imprinted all over its rind.

Pecorino cheese Originally a sheep's milk cheese, pecorino is sharper and more piquant than Parmesan. There are different styles, e.g Pecorino Sardo and Pecorino Romano.

Polenta The grain, made from maize (corn), is usually a coarse yellow meal but it is also ground to a fine white flour. It is sometimes labelled *farina gialla* or *granoturco*. The dish polenta is basically the grain cooked and formed into a loaf.

Porcini Mushrooms (*Funghi porcini*) The Italian cepes or *Boletus Edulis* mushroom with a woody flavour, usually sold dried in small packets or in bulk. These need to be reconstituted in warm water for 30 minutes before use. When fresh, during a brief season, they are rich and succulent.

Prosciutto (Prosciutto crudo) Uncooked, unsmoked ham which has been salted and air-cured. Available on the bone, boned, or pre-sliced. It should be sweet and succulent, not salty and dry. Sometimes called Parma ham, although all prosciutto is not neccessarily from there.

Ricotta cheese A fresh cheese made from the whey of separated milk, unmatured and unsmoked ricotta has a life of 4 to 5 days.

Saffron (*Zafferano*) The bright orange dried stamens of the crocus flower. It is available in small sachets or vials, in powdered form or in strands. If using the strands, the flavour will intensify if they are first lightly toasted, or alternately, steeped in a little warm water.

INDEX